The Motivating Team Leader

DR. LEWIS E. LOSONCY

To Randy,
Lew Losoncy

S^{t}_{L}

St. Lucie Press
Delray Beach, Florida

Printed and bound in the U.S.A. Printed on acid-free paper.
10 9 8 7 6 5 4 3 2 1

Library of Congress Cataloging-in-Publication Data

Losoncy, Lewis E.
    The motivating team leader / by Lewis Losoncy.
      p.   cm.
    Includes bibliographical references and index.
    ISBN 1-884015-82-4 (pbk.)
    1. Employee motivation. 2. Work groups. I. Title.
HF5549.5.M63L67 1995
658.3′14—dc20   94-46380
                                                           CIP

Direct all inquiries to St. Lucie Press, Inc., 100 E. Linton Blvd., Suite 403B, Delray Beach, Florida 33483.
Phone: (407) 274-9906
Fax: (407) 274-9927

S^{t}_{L}

Published by
St. Lucie Press
100 E. Linton Blvd., Suite 403B
Delray Beach, FL 33483

*Have you ever noticed that
the only ones who ever reach their dreams
are those who have them!*

*Never make the mistake
of limiting the visions of your future
by the narrow experiences of your past.*

*One person with a dream
becomes a majority
in any size group*

*The motivating leader is that one person
with a dream for the future.*

*You are that one-person majority
who has a dream to empower your team
from your limited past, to your unlimited future!*

IS THIS BOOK FOR YOU?

Are you highly motivated yourself
but find that your success today
depends upon the motivation of other people?

Are you extremely busy
and in need of some practical approaches
to motivate others—immediately?

Do you prefer using a positive approach
rather than constant pushing
to get your team moving?

Would you like to go beyond
just the financial motivators to include
the psychological, social, self-actualizing,
and inspirational motivators?

If so, then you are ready to become
The Motivating Team Leader!

DEDICATION

With Love to

My wife Diane,
my leadership example and researcher,

And our daughter and motivator, Gabrielle

CONTENTS

ACKNOWLEDGMENTS

In loving memory of both my mother, Anna Losoncy, and to my father, Lew, a person who no one in the world has ever said a bad word about. You both were my initial motivating leaders.

To Arnie Miller, co-founder of Matrix Essentials and now its spiritual leader, who taught us to think, believe, dream, and dare. Together we moved 55,000 Twins fans to yell our newest product, VaVoom, at the seventh game of the 1987 World Series.

To Sydell Miller, co-founder of Matrix, whose creative leadership is revolutionizing the pride and prosperity in the beauty profession with her all-embracing concept of Total Image Consulting.

To Mike DeGennaro, Matrix's President, whose leadership, vision, strength, insight, and foresight are true reflections of the original, unchanged, solid dream of the founding father and mother.

The Motivating Team Leader proudly acknowledges the Matrix Motivating Leadership Team:

Dennis Lubin, simply the finest innovative marketing man in the industry.

Dave Cook, the Matrix "numbers person," whose emphasis is on the latter word. Put Ph.D. behind your name.

Jeff Kunz, who led the Matrix plant's growth more like a horticulturist than a gardener.

Bob Miller, whose extensive background and experience give him a deep understanding of the implications of sales on every aspect of the salon industry.

Sara Jones, the mover and shaker, the momentum maker, the finder-of-a-way of Matrix, who simply sees the need and fills it.

R.W. Miller, a solid citizen of Matrix culture.

Stacie Halpern, whose strength and innovation bring the dream into clearer focus.

Jody Bryne, third generation futurist of the beauty industry.

Craig Miller, Diana Reed Sandonato, Carole Walderman, and Nancy Hershey, for putting wings on the Total Image Dream.

And Shawn Clary and Tracy Menafee, for selling people on themselves.

To Linda Piazza and Robin Grider, two of many Matrix "get-it-doners."

To our Matrix field force, the most motivating leadership team ever assembled in the beauty profession.

To the visionaries at St. Lucie Press, including President Dennis Buda, who believed, and Sandy Pearlman, who found a way.

To Andrea Gates, the optimistic data processor who got things done. With that quality, you could work anywhere in the world.

ABOUT THE AUTHOR

Lewis Losoncy is a psychologist and the author of ten books on encouragement, success, leadership, and teamwork, including *Turning People On, You Can Do It,* and *Teamwork Makes the Dream Work.*

Dr. Losoncy is responsible for building an Encouraging Team at Matrix Essentials (Solon, Ohio), North America's largest manufacturer of professional-only beauty products.

He has appeared on numerous TV and radio programs, including CNN and CBS's "This Morning," and has been featured in assorted print media, from *The Wall Street Journal* to *Psychology Today.*

Dr. Losoncy has lectured in all fifty states, most of the Canadian provinces, and throughout Australia and New Zealand.

INTRODUCTION

Who was the greatest motivating team leader you ever experienced? What did this person do to inspire your team? What particular approaches did he or she use to encourage you to lift yourself to higher levels of vision and performance? This person was a human stimulant who knew how to bring out the best in you and your teammates.

In contrast, think of the most discouraging team leader you ever experienced. How did these two leaders, or influences on the team's destiny, differ in their approach to people? It was their motivational style that made the difference.

The fact is that the most vital task of the leader is to motivate, inspire, empower, and encourage the team's primary resource—the unlimited, creative human potential—to find better ways. In *21st Century Leadership*, Kenneth Chenault wrote, "What is clearly going to be needed in the 21st Century, particularly with the diversity in the work force, is the ability to inspire...Inspirational leadership is going to become very critical." The authors of the same book observed, "As we spoke with leaders, we were impressed by the sensitivity many of them displayed about the human aspect of leadership. Words like *courage, hope, caring, heart, compassion, listening, cooperation, and service* kept cropping up. This should not be surprising, given the shift towards empowerment and

1

bringing out the best in people" (McFarland, Senn, and Childress, 1993).

This book on motivating leadership starts where every success story begins—with *courage.*

Motivating Leaders Bring Out the Team Members' Courage to Believe in Themselves

Winston Churchill asserted that if he could have only one quality, it would be *courage,* because with courage he could acquire all other qualities. The motivating team leader uses en-*courage*-ment to stimulate team members to have the courage to believe in themselves. Belief raises standards and goals. Belief generates optimism and determination. Belief creates positive expectations and intrinsic motivation. The team with the courage to believe takes action.

In considering the power of belief, the philosopher Spinoza asserted that "For as long as a person believes a certain task to be impossible, for that exact period of time it will be impossible." But the very moment a person believes the dream is possible is the exact moment when the person (or the team) moves forward.

Have you ever noticed that the only people who ever achieve their dreams are those who have a dream? The team with the courage to believe in a new dream has a tremendous buoyant advantage. They are uplifted by their shared vision, and together they proceed confidently, expecting to succeed. They act differently. They feel differently. They think differently.

Bertrand Russell reinforced the solid ground the optimist stands on when he asserted, "In the vast realm of the alive, creative mind, there are no limitations." The disbeliever, on the other hand, stands on shaky ground. As John Dryden concluded, "When there is no hope, there can be no endeavor." This is the destiny and downward direction lived out by the discouraged person.

In *Learned Optimism,* psychologist Martin Seligman (1991) reveals that a person's beliefs about his or her setbacks (explanatory style) are the main determinant as to whether the person remains motivated to go forward or gives up. The motivating leader encourages the team to view setbacks with an optimistic explanatory style; that is, setbacks are situation-related, rather than reflections of personal failures, and are temporary rather than permanent.

There is a direct connection between the motivating team leader's encouragement and whether or not the team develops the courage to believe.

Team leader's encouragement =
Team's courage to believe

There is also a clear positive relationship between a team's courage to believe and its eventual achievements:

Courage to believe = Raised standards and goals
Optimism
Determination
Elevated achievements

Estimates of how much of our total creative potential we use range from 2 to 15 percent. The major reason why we function at the lower range is simply *discouragement,* with its accompanying symptoms of anxiety, fear, blocking, passive-aggressiveness, rebellion, uncooperativeness, pessimism, and self-defeatism.

Motivating leaders are those who create encouraging conditions for their team members in order to bring out more of their measureless, unused human potential. It was said that Walt Disney could wring out the creativity from his artists' minds long after they thought their ideas had dried up. One could say that he helped people go a step beyond to make Fantasyland a real place on a map. John Kennedy had the ability to motivate a nation of people to ask what they could do for their land. Mother

Theresa inspired the world by giving nourishment to the hearts of people. Martin Luther King, Jr. added some new dimensions to the way a society looks at itself.

These leaders, and many others, had something in common. They all had the ability to move people on to greater achievements, to appeal to the highest motives in people, to help everyone feel like an involved, contributing team member—and to use a greater percentage of their cerebral possibilities. The leadership techniques of the great motivators are relevant to anyone whose success depends upon the performance of others.

The Motivating Leader Reinforces Cultural Values, Articulates Vision, and Empowers the Team's Human Resources— And Then Gets Out of Their Way

Whether or not a team fulfills its potential is related to leadership's grasp, definition, articulation, modeling, and reinforcement of the team's *culture*. The culture is composed of the common underlying values by which the team collectively lives as it does its business. A strong, clearly articulated culture brings cohesiveness to the team. It is the team's cement. The leader's role is to provide the cultural cement among the teammates. A shared culture can provide a source of pride in being unique and different from other defined or undefined cultures. The leader unifies the team members through an awareness of their common culture and shows how community creates opportunity for all. In other words, *come-unity* creates opport-*unity*. If every teammate knows, for example, that his or her culture believes in and values "exceeding customer expectations," the team proceeds as one and sends a clear, unambiguous message to the consumer.

The culture flows from the leader's *vision*. Vision is the leader's dream that stretches the team's imagination and pride to their limits. Whereas vision illuminates where the team is going, culture is the collection of common ways the team will use to get there. For example, leadership vision that emphasizes zero defects or service quality, if constantly reinforced and rallied around as a cultural standard, defines the team's destination—and its destiny.

The leader also *empowers* the team. Empowerment involves espousing the vision; defining the culture; encouraging by re-engineering the team's self-image through emphasizing its strengths, assets, and resources; and then getting out of the way.

General issues such as downsizing or benchmarking and more specific issues like dealing with difficult or discouraged people, conflicts, cliques, or even violence on the team are all laid at the door of the leader. Such issues are best resolved if the leader has the skills to cope with disharmonious situations or discouragement on the team. The leader needs the skills to encourage.

On Which Teams Will You Be the Motivating Leader?

Whether you call yourself a leader, a manager, a president or vice-president, a coach, a parent, a teacher, an administrator, or even a shepherd of a flock, your most important resource is your people. And the most crucial determinant of your success is your ability to inspire, motivate, and encourage your human resources.

Who on your team could use some motivation and encouragement? Who is discouraged and has lost the courage to believe and the desire to achieve? You, the motivating leader, will make the difference, whether at your next session, a staff meeting, or over your next cup of coffee together.

You will soon have a total motivational and encouragement strategy, one that goes way beyond the important financial motivators. You will learn 43 practical approaches that motivate by fulfilling the psychological, the social, the professional, and the inspirational needs of your teammates.

The motivating leader reaches both deeper and higher than the traditional manager. In discussing the clear distinction between a leader and a manager, Jack Hawley (1993) wrote that "Managers manage people and the human effort. Leaders focus on the deeper, non-physical dimension—energy, heart and spirit. Managers deal in organizational form, leaders embrace the unified culture and community."

Do you have the courage to believe in yourself and in your team? Leadership is encouraging and inspiring your people to "catch it," like the 1969 Mets, 1980 U.S. Olympic Hockey Team, or the 1994 Brazilian World Cup Team.

Why Do Leaders and Teams Fail?
How Can Leaders and Teams Succeed?

A skilled, creative hair designer is promoted to the position of managing a twelve-person beauty salon. With an excellent formal background in styling hair and some on-the-job training in specific areas such as compensation systems, reading profit-and-loss statements, retailing, and appointment scheduling, she eagerly faces her new challenge. Not long after she receives her manager name tag, the "people" part of her job starts to whittle away her will. She lacks skills in leadership and assertiveness with people, and the staff starts to tread all over her like an un-welcome mat. The stress that her lack of motivation skills causes is transformed into psychological symptoms. Insomnia, anxiety attacks, and headaches become as much a part of her life as is her job. After a period of only four months, the formerly successful cosmetologist leaves not only her management position but, sadly, her profession.

This unfortunate leadership story could have been rewritten if this manager had developed:

1. A take-charge attitude toward her team in order to gain their cooperation and respect

2. A strategy to minimize employee problems through setting up policies and procedures

3. A systematic approach to steer problem employees onto a constructive path

4. The self-encouragement to keep her own head up and even enjoy the challenge of encouraging others

The ambitious middle-aged manager of a fast-food restaurant supervises mostly young adults in her seven day-a-week operation. She can't believe the irresponsibility she sees in her minimum-wage employees. Tardiness and absence are almost daily occurrences, and she is at her wit's end in trying to find a way to motivate these kids to take on more responsibility. The well-intentioned but frustrated leader argues that "kids nowadays don't want to work like we did."

The fast-food manager needs to develop new skills to motivate the youngsters of today. To become a motivating leader, she needs to acquire:

1. Approaches to encourage her young workers on the team to be responsible, motivated, and productive employees

2. A plan to help her people not only to deal with everyday problems but to learn to anticipate other possible problems

3. Skills in hiring new employees and skills in setting limits, as well as facing the task of firing individuals who sabotage the team's efforts

A husband and wife sign up to start their own family business on a part-time, and hopefully someday on a full-time, basis. They firmly believe in their product and want to spread their fervor. They earn a commission on the sales of everyone they enlist to sell the product. While most people initially "catch fire" to their ideas, they find that most also quickly "burn out." They soon realize that their business success is related not just to their own product knowledge, but to their skills in motivating others as well.

This couple's business could have been successful if they had developed:

1. An approach to win people over

2. Skills in building a team of responsible, intrinsically motivated self-starters who can function without continually being pushed

3. A system to build pride in their people to increase their productivity

A spirited saleslady moves up the ranks to the position of sales manager like a helium balloon under water. This highly competitive manager argues that the way to motivate people is to play one teammate against another. She believes that the way to get people "moving" is to constantly highlight outstanding performance with charts, public recognition, and free vacations. After all, the emphasis on competition worked with her, and it works with about 15 percent of the team. On what appears to her to be a side issue, the sales manager notices backbiting, sabotaging, jealousy, excessive excuse making, bickering over territories, the development of cliques, and poor morale in the large remaining portion of the sales force. She wonders why "our team" doesn't work together, cooperate, and share ideas.

With some practical help, this sales manager could develop:

1. A plan to build team power, whereby everyone works together as a cooperative, helpful unit

2. A strategy to increase the sales productivity of all teammates rather than just a few

3. Approaches to encourage everyone to channel competitive energies where they belong—against the competition and not against one another

A high school football coach, who is a talented strategist and was a trophy-winning quarterback in his university years, doesn't understand why his players are so apathetic. When he used the hard-nosed approach, he lost his top two players, who complained, "We don't need this hassle." He has switched to a softer approach, but thinks he has lost his team's respect. The coach doesn't know where to turn, but he knows that unless he improves morale, and his win–loss record, he won't be asked back the following year.

This coach can become a motivating team leader if he develops:

1. An understanding of how to motivate people to want to give it their all

2. The self-confidence to be goal-centered and not ego-centered

3. Skills in building team spirit to increase morale

The salon manager, the fast-food manager, the husband and wife with the family business, the sales manager, and the coach all have many assets that elevated them to their leadership positions, and they all are highly motivated individuals. But the future success of each of these leaders depends upon factors outside of themselves— the motivation and performance of their teams. They need new approaches, strategies, and techniques to build a team with a winning attitude, with the desire to cooperate and with the courage to believe in themselves and the team.

Helping you acquire the encouraging strategies of the motivating leader is the goal of this book.

1

THE MOTIVATING LEADER'S PRIMARY TOOL: ENCOURAGEMENT

Have you ever noticed how you can get a sense of the style of a manager or leader just by observing a sampling of his or her employees or teammates?

It's true! Just as the floating leaves of fall hint of the presence of nearby trees, the attitudes of the people in an organization whisper about the leader's style. Each day provides dozens of opportunities for you to observe the common threads that run through the teammates in their various roles and responsibilities. These common threads may be thought of as parts of the team's woven culture. The articulation and reinforcement of the team's culture, defined by some as "the way we do things around here," is the responsibility of leadership. Failure to define and reward cultural values leaves the culture random, lacking unity and cohesion.

Wherever you do business, you can probably consciously or subconsciously sense "how things are done around here." We all have a natural tendency to generalize about the total organization based on the attitude and behavior of the few members we meet. Such generalization is, more often than not, accurate.

Your Out-of-Town Hotel Experience:
A Motivating Leader Behind the Scenes?

Imagine that you have just weathered a stormy five-hour coast-to-coast flight. Your body is still shaking like a tuning fork as you await the faceless, nameless limo driver from Hotel Unknown located in a city that has never lived in the cozy areas of your mind. Your comfortable feelings are as lost as your baggage.

The driver from the hotel arrives, steps out of the van, and greets you with a big smile. His warm, helpful actions overpower the evening chill. The understanding style of this enthusiastic youth may not only be telling you that he is sensitive, but perhaps so is his hotel leader, and perhaps a sensitive customer style is part of the whole culture you will soon be experiencing.

Next, you encounter the helpful, sympathetic, cheerful, courteous young girl at the hotel registration desk. By her compassionate manner, she reinforces your prophesy for a pleasant visit while in the comfortable care of this hotel's customer-sensitive team.

The limo driver and the clerk are your first indications, your leading clues at this point, that the hotel is customer responsive. Your senses, once potentially explosive from the hectic pace, are delicately detonated by employee empathy. Your out-of-town anxieties lose their argument. The crystal ball in your mind tells you that you will be able to get to work on the things you are there to work on. You get a comforting feeling as you kick off your shoes and relax in your new home away from home.

This hotel is no longer a stranger to you because of its motivated team. Each teammate you meet with the same winning style is further proof that your experience was not a result of random, haphazard events. The positive people were a result of the real hero behind the scenes—the motivating team leader.

Should I Share My Idea to Improve Our Team? It All Depends on the Leader's Style!

The leader's style is the unparalleled reason why teammates are involved in developing and sharing more effective and efficient ideas for the team's growth. Whether or not a team member has the courage to share a new idea and feels important enough to contribute, or even cares enough to offer a suggestion, is related to that individual's perception of his or her leader.

In a discouraging atmosphere, teammates hold their ideas back, as children do when they are afraid to raise their hands at school in the presence of a discouraging teacher. In an encouraging atmosphere, on the other hand, creative ideas and suggestions for improvement flow like the high tide.

Consider the following imaginary meeting that might have taken place decades ago in the creative department of a toy manufacturing company. The goal of the session was to generate ideas for future products. There certainly was no lack of ideas among the divergent thinking minds. The only thing missing was the courage to express those ideas because of how previous creative ideas were received.

"Should I share my new thought today, or will the manager make a sarcastic, discouraging remark about my idea for a new toy?" wondered one anxious employee. Many teammates wondered the same thing. Red and green lights flashed on and off intermittently in the anxious employee's mind based on, more than anything else, his perception of the manager's reaction.

Today the manager is smiling. He starts by inspiring

his team. "The only bad idea is the idea that isn't shared this morning. The idea sitting in your mind right now could be the big one, the cornerstone of our company's future. At worst, we won't be able to use your idea at this time. So there is no risk in sharing your creative ideas for our new toys for the spring."

The anxious employee, encouraged by the motivating leader's words, raises his hand and suggests, "Well, I have this idea about creating a toy that would be extremely inexpensive to manufacture, easy to package, and is novel. You see, I call this idea a 'pet rock.' It could..."

The manager's style made the difference!

Eight Goals that Motivating, Encouraging Leaders Accomplish

Why be an encouraging leader? The encouraging leader can more effectively achieve eight primary goals through his or her team that discouraging leaders cannot.

- **Goal 1: Communication.** The encouraging leader creates an atmosphere of mutual understanding and respect for everyone's roles and responsibilities. Aren't misunderstandings and disrespect the primary reasons for disharmony?

- **Goal 2: Team building.** The encouraging leader builds teammates by being a positive influence who recognizes individual and group potential. Discouraging leaders actually believe that you build people up by tearing them down.

- **Goal 3: Giving meaning and purpose.** The encouraging leader combats burnout and lifts teammates out of a rut by giving meaning to what they do. Discouraging leaders assume that a paycheck is the only reason why people work and consequently miss out on much of their teams' potential sources of motivation, such as inspirational needs.

- **Goal 4: Winning team feeling.** The encouraging leader increases productivity by conveying positive expectations or a "we can do it" esprit de corps. Did you ever have a leader who had no confidence in you and your abilities? How did you perform in that discouraging setting?

- **Goal 5: Confront with class.** The encouraging leader has the skills to constructively steer the discouraged teammate back onto the productive path. Discouraging leaders use the name-calling, put-down approach because it occasionally works—temporarily.

- **Goal 6: Find a way.** The encouraging leader is both a realist and an optimist who encourages the team to face realistic challenges head on and then mobilize their unlimited artistic, creative minds to find a way to meet them. Discouraging leaders make the mistake of either wishing things were different or believing that problems have no solutions, either of which results in frustration.

- **Goal 7: Enhanced morale through involvement.** The encouraging leader skillfully knows how to tap the creative minds of the team members, thus increasing morale through everyone's involvement. Discouraging leaders squash ideas with "that'll never work here" or "you must be kidding," thus producing apathy, division, or uncooperativeness.

- **Goal 8: Turn individuals into a winning team.** The encouraging leader emphasizes cooperation over competition and values everyone's contribution to the team's outcomes.

You can be the motivating team leader who achieves these goals and others by drawing on the rich ideas from many sources in the study of the use of encouragement to bring out a team's potential.

The Encouraging Leader Senses the Teammates' Social Needs

The primary influence in the study of encouragement is Alfred Adler, the common-sense psychiatrist who believed that human motivation could best be understood by viewing it in its "social context."

Have you ever found that you are more creative around some people than others? Why? You were the same person in both social contexts, weren't you? According to Adler, you actually were not because in an encouraging social context you are more courageous, which brings out more of your creative potential.

Adler believed that in order for a person's actions and attitudes to be accurately understood, they need to be observed in the context of a unique social setting. As our social environment changes, we change, and our potential opens and closes in rhythm with the amount of encouragement or discouragement we experience.

Adler also argued that a person's primary needs seek fulfillment in the social setting. We have needs to contribute, belong, and strive for significance, as well as needs for attention and recognition.

In *The Encouragement Book,* Don Dinkmeyer and Lewis Losoncy highlight the influential role of encouragement by concluding:

> Every time two people come in contact, both individuals are influenced to move in a more "turned-on," encouraged direction or in a "turned-off," discouraged one. When we are discouraged, we tend to discourage. And when we discourage others, we become more discouraged ourselves. By the same token, because we are social beings, when we encourage someone else, we are encouraged as we realize the positive

contribution we can make in helping others develop their "inner courage." This is certainly contrary to the popular notion that the more we put other people down, the more we pick ourselves up.

Today, encouragement is the key ingredient in all personal and professional relationships. Did you ever have a doctor who was quite knowledgeable about medicine but had a poor bedside manner or was even discouraging or insensitive to your needs as a patient? Or did you ever have a teacher whose brilliance was obvious, but was miles above and beyond the students? You probably felt intimidated and yes...discouraged. You learned more from a less intelligent teacher–leader, who had empathy for you and encouraged you, didn't you? (Dinkmeyer and Losoncy, 1995)

Optimistically, encouraging leaders can help fulfill the social needs of teammates by developing the Mutual Encouragement Skills presented in the program *Teamwork Makes the Dream Work* (L. Losoncy, 1994). Research by Diane Losoncy (1994) has found that by developing the skills of mutual encouragement offered in this program, teammates experience an increase in feelings of teamness. Teamness is a concept detailed by Jay Hall (1988). Losoncy also found that mutual encouragement skills training can increase team members' social self-concepts (D. Losoncy, 1994).

In other words, an encouraging leader can provide conditions that will fulfill the team's social needs as they relate to the team's productivity, cohesiveness, identity, and affiliation. In addition, the leader can also provide Mutual Encouragement Skill development opportunities that will lead to both increased sense of teamness and social self-concept.

The encouraging leader is sensitive to fulfilling each teammate's social needs and recognizes that these needs are an important part of a total encouragement strategy. At no time in history has it been more important to develop a sense of community (*come-unity*) than today.

The Encouraging Leader Senses
the Teammates' Inspirational Needs

In "Creating Esprit de Corps," contributor Jim Channon writes sensitively about the "organization as community" to fulfill not only the *social* but the *spiritual* needs of its membership:

> When people had tribes to go home to, or villages where they could share their seasonal festival, or even neighborhoods with some personal intimacy, these more spirit evoking elements of culture were part of a natural order of life. But, as we approach the 21st century, our business cultures have become our "tribes"—our villages and neighborhoods. They are the building blocks that will shape our planetary culture. Our older social cultures have become atomized by communications technology and commuting and have largely disappeared as a consequence. So if there is no experience of spirit in corporations, there may not be much spirit in the civilization at large (Channon, 1992).

Decades ago, psychiatrist Erich Fromm foresaw the implications of technology on the human spirit. Were dehumanization and alienation inevitable in a world where people become reduced to numbers? Fromm concluded that the major task of the 21st century society was to "humanize our technological world."

In *Care of the Soul,* Thomas Moore provides the reader with a deeper view about the relationship between work and soul:

> We move closer to the soul's work when we go deeper than intellectual abstraction and imaginary fancies that do not well up from the more profound roots of feeling. The more deeply our work stirs imagination and corresponds to images that lie there at the bedrock of identity and fate, the more it will have soul. Work is an attempt to find an adequate alchemy that

both wakens and satisfies the very root of being. Most of us put a great deal of time into work, not only because we have to work so many hours to make a living, but because work is central to the soul's opus (work as imagination) (Moore, 1994, p. 185).

The Encouraging Leader Senses the Teammates' Self-Actualization Growth Needs

In addition to fulfilling part of a person's social and spiritual needs, the encouraging leader draws upon the ideas of Abraham Maslow, who studied the healthiest, most fulfilled humans. Maslow called these outstanding specimens "self-actualizers." He rebelled against studying unhappy or unhealthy people and then generalizing from those who are not fulfilling their possibilities onto the total human condition.

In his book entitled *The Farther Reaches of Human Nature,* Maslow wrote:

> If you want to answer the question how tall can the human species grow, then obviously it is well to pick out the ones who are already the tallest and study them. If we want to know how fast a human can run, then it is no use to average out the speed of a sample of the population; it is far better to collect Olympic gold medal winners and see how well they can do. If we want to know the possibilities for spiritual growth, value growth or moral development in human beings, then I maintain that we can learn the most by studying our most moral, ethical or saintly people (Maslow, 1971).

The desire of the motivating leader is to create an encouraging atmosphere that invites each teammate's courage to actualize his or her fuller creative potential. Maslow believed that disease and apathy were the result of stifling our actualization needs.

One result of an encouraging team environment is that each person's energies are used in constructive versus defensive, destructive activities. You might say that each teammate gets more out of each moment, or what Mihaly Csikszentmihaly calls "flow."

In his book on the subject, *Flow: The Psychology of Optimal Experiences,* the author describes flow as "the state in which people are so involved in an activity that nothing else seems to matter; the experience itself is so enjoyable that people will do it, even at great cost for the sheer sake of doing it" (1990, p. 2).

The author's research demonstrates that flow is possible while engaged in work. Curiously, flow often is not associated with easy moments, but rather with moments of great challenge. Csikszentmihaly observed:

> Contrary to what we usually believe, moments (of flow) the best moments in our lives, are not the passive, receptive and relaxing times—although such experiences can also be enjoyable, if we have worked hard to attain them. The best moments usually occur when a person's body or mind is stretched to its limits in a voluntary effort to accomplish something difficult or worthwhile. Optimal experience is something we can make happen. For a child it could be placing, with trembling fingers, the last block on a tower she has built, higher than any built before so far...For each person there are thousands of opportunities, challenges to expand ourselves.
>
> Such experiences are not necessarily pleasant at the time they occur. The swimmer's muscles might have ached during his most memorable race, his lungs might have felt like exploding...yet these could have been the best moment of his life (1990, pp. 3–4).

Moments of flow are often moments of great challenge and are also great moments of freedom to get more out of each experience. Flow is facilitated by an encouraging leader.

The Encouraging Leader Senses
the Power of Team Synergy

Some teams are basically a collection of individuals; other teams are synergized. Experience the difference:

A collection of individuals   A synergized team

$1 + 1 + 1 + 1 + 1 = 5$ $1 \times 2 \times 3 \times 4 \times 5 = 120$

Mark Twain described synergy as "the bonus that is achieved when things works together harmoniously." Do you have some friends who you just click with? When you are together, your creative juices flow, and together you come up with ideas that you may not have created alone. That bonus is synergy. As shown in the above equation comparing a collection of individuals and a synergized team, the interplay of five synergized teammates creates a multiple synergy.

In *Teamwork Makes the Dream Work,* Losoncy concludes:

> The science of team dynamics has shown that the whole team will produce...either more or less...than what a bunch of individuals will produce alone, depending upon the way the individual parts of the team work together. Team synergy is the bonus that is achieved when all parts of a team encourage each other to work together to achieve their shared dream.
>
> Winning teams rarely happen by chance or luck. Winning teams are the results of commitments of individuals to rise above their own self-interest or cliquish interest and become Mutual Encouragers. The collective spirit of encouraging winning teams is experienced when each teammate makes the commitment to bring out the best in each other by living the 7 Principles of Mutual Encouragement.

The 7 Principles of Mutual Encouragement:

Principle 1   **Synergy:** "All of us together can do much more than each of us can do alone"

Principle 2   **Cooperation:** "Cooperating multiplies us, competing divides us"

Principle 3   **Focus:** "Determining our destination determines our destiny"

Principle 4   **Respect:** "Centering on our strengths builds our force"

Principle 5   **Realism:** "What is, is!"

Principle 6   **Optimism:** "Believing problems have solutions gives us the advantage"

Principle 7   **Progress:** "Encouraging progress precedes praising success" (L. Losoncy, 1994)

The encouraging leader's major task is to turn self-centered individuals into synergized teammates. In *Team Players and Teamwork,* Glenn Parker (1990) describes four individual team player styles: (1) contributor, (2) collaborator, (3) communicator, and (4) challenger. In *Team Building,* Peter Mears and Frank Voehl (1994) argue that nothing less than a whole new mindset of rising above self-centered thinking to team thinking is vital for the motivating leader to instill in the team. Rex Gatto (1992) addresses the importance of flexibility in leading teams in today's changing work world in his book entitled *Teamwork through Flexible Leadership.*

All of these sources for becoming an encouraging leader are essential to read, understand, and use. There is an additional foundation to develop these approaches to becoming a motivating, encouraging leader. Over a period of four years, I asked groups of individuals in the United States, Canada, Australia, and New Zealand to record the qualities, strategies, or "ways of being" that were present in the motivating leaders in their lives. I found that everyone had expertise in understanding the difference between discouragement and encouragement from their own history. The following two exercises can help you identify the qualities of discouragers and encouragers in your own life.

Personal Experience Exercise to Identify Characteristics of Discouraging Leaders

Think of some discouraging leaders from your past. List a few characteristics, traits, or "ways of being" that were present in their actions or attitudes. Your response can be global ("this person rarely listened") or specific ("when I started on the job, he didn't even introduce me to anyone").

1. _____

2. _____

3. _____

4. _____

5. _____

The following are some responses given to the same question you just answered: What were some of the characteristics of the most discouraging leader you experienced? (Responses are recorded exactly as they were given.) Are there any similarities to your responses?

1. Always pointed out what I was doing wrong, never what I did right.

2. Never listened.

3. Had double standards, one for his favorites—another for the others.

4. Know it all.

5. Stole ideas.

6. No time for you.

7. Didn't trust you.

8. Talked down.

9. Gave false hopes.

10. Belittled you.

11. Made you feel like an underdog.

12. Took advantage of you.

13. Gave only negative feedback.

14. Set up inconsistent rules.

15. Lied.

16. Would fly off the handle. You lived in fear when he was around.

17. Took on all the responsibilities. You felt like you were unimportant.

18. Used their position to overpower you.

19. Gave no direction. I didn't even know what doing a good job meant.

20. Would say things like, "I'll see you in my office after work," first thing in the morning.

21. Intimidated.

22. Put your ideas down.

23. Keeps laying extra things on you to do and not even being considerate enough to ask for your help or say "thank you."

24. Negative attitude.

25. Saw you as important only as someone who produced. Not as a person.

26. Compared you to other people.

27. Made you feel unwanted—like at staff meetings never even looked at you.

28. Smooth talker, but no substance.

29. Never satisfied, nit-picker.

30. Would show you how much he produced when he was in your job before you were.

31. Always had to get the last word in.

32. Would make you take his responsibilities, like dealing with tough, angry customers.

33. Would yell at you in front of others. I felt so small.

34. Played favorites.

35. Would socialize with the men and not the women. It gave the men the edge for promotions.

36. Critical facial expressions, like heavy eyebrows.

37. Close-minded.

38. You'd bat your brains out working and it was never even noticed.

39. Used sarcasm and embarrassment.

40. Assumed I knew what he wanted or what he was thinking.

And, finally, one of the most interesting responses: "I just knew that Johnny Paycheck worked for this guy before he wrote 'Take this job and shove it.'"

Were any of these responses similar to yours? If so, you may have found a pattern that is present in discouragers.

Personal Experience Exercise to
Identify Characteristics of Encouragers

Think of some encouraging leaders you experienced in your past. List some of their characteristics, traits, or "ways of being" with people.

1 _____

2. _____

3. _____

4. _____

5. _____

Now compare your conclusions with the experiences of others. Again, look for patterns.

1. Listened to you, really listened.

2. Respected your abilities, believed in you.

3. Saw what you did right as well as pointing out what you did wrong.

4. Could delegate responsibility.

5. Enthusiasm.

6. Sense of humor.

7. Admitted mistakes himself.

8. Gave you credit for your ideas.

9. Could recognize when you needed a lift and was there for you.

10. Interested in you as a person.

11. Was at peace with himself.

12. Consistent.

13. Good teacher, willing to share ideas.

14. Criticized constructively.

15. Followed through on promises.

16. Honest, genuine, real.

17. Positive.

18. Permitted freedom and independence as long as you got your job done. You didn't feel smothered or claustrophobic.

19. Gave you a feeling that things you said in confidence would be kept in confidence.

20. Said "hello" or "glad to see you" in the morning.

21. I'd hear comments from my manager's boss to me like, "Bob tells me you're doing a great job." What a lift that would give me.

22. Accepted me even if I pointed out how things could be better in the department or if I criticized him.

23. She showed you how what you did was important to the company. It really motivated me to see that my job was significant.

24. Helped me feel like part of a team.

25. Did little things like reassure me when I came back from vacation that I was missed.

26. I knew exactly what was expected of me.

27. I felt very creative around him. If he didn't like my idea, he would still appreciate my efforts.

28. My first day on the job he took me around to meet everybody and I felt immediately accepted.

29. Fair but firm.

30. Vulnerable and would share his own shortcomings.

31. He would always be available to talk to. Gave you time.

32. Believed in me. I felt special and unique, but so did everybody else.

33. Would remember our conversations.

34. Open-minded to new ideas.

35. Non-defensive.

36. Gave good leadership. Could lift the team's spirits. Saw obstacles as challenges.

37. Was a terrific example. I even quit smoking and started dieting after her example. She was a total person.

38. Professional—never backbiting or putting down people. Even when he was attacked he listened and rationally explained his position.

39. Warm, but not a warmth stemming from weakness.

40. After disciplining you, he gave you hope and a new start.

Are these ideas consistent with your own about the style of an encourager?

Discouragers and encouragers differ in their approach to people. The following checklist can be used as a quick reminder to keep yourself on the encouraging track and to keep your team highly motivated because of the courage to believe.

Keep this checklist with you as a reminder during times when you observe unmotivated people to help you find ways to lift them.

A Leader's Checklist of Strategies to Encourage

Tends to discourage	Neither discouraging nor encouraging	Tends to encourage
1. I tend to talk too much and not listen enough. (Ch. 3)		I spend a great deal of time listening to my people.
2. My attitude at work has been negative lately. (Chs. 5, 8, 9)		I have a positive, optimistic attitude toward my work and my people
3. I have been spending more time on what my people do wrong than on what they do correctly. (Ch. 4)		I make a conscious effort to point out the things that my people do right as well as wrong.
4. I haven't recently shown each of my people why his or her work is important. (Ch. 5)		I believe that each one of my employees knows how meaningful his or her contribution is.
5. I make all of the decisions. (Chs. 9, 10)		I involve my people in most of the decisions on how we can most effectively achieve the organization's goals.
6. I think my people would probably say that I am only interested in them as producers, not people. (Ch. 3)		I'm genuinely interested in my people's lives and have a good feel for each person's individual long-term goals.

A Leader's Checklist of Strategies to Encourage

	Tends to discourage	*Neither discouraging nor encouraging*	*Tends to encourage*
7.	I tend to be closed-minded to new ideas or ways of doing things. (Chs. 3, 9, 10)		I am open-minded toward my people's ideas.
8.	My people rarely bring me new ideas. (Chs. 8, 9, 10)		I can count on new ideas from people daily.
9.	My people see me as a perfectionist. (Chs. 3, 9, 10)		When an employee makes a mistake, it is not a catastrophe, so we simply correct it and set up a system so that it minimizes the chance of it happening again.
10.	When a new employee arrives, I haven't been sensitive to that "anxious first day feeling." I just put the person on the job without any preparation. (Chs. 3, 5)		When a new employee starts, I listen to his or her feelings about the job, provide a safe atmosphere where the person can ask questions, and introduce the person to each staff member.
11.	When an employee is absent for a period of time or takes a vacation, I just assume that he or she can come back on the job without a welcome. (Ch. 3)		I am sensitive to the feelings a person has when being away from work for a while.

I believe that my people trust me.

When I discipline people, I tell them very specifically why they are being disciplined, what I specifically expect from them, and I show my belief that they can improve.

I am a positive leader who communicates a "we can do it" attitude.

I try to treat everyone equally.

I feel that if everyone followed my work habits, things would be better.

I discipline and confront my discouraged, unproductive people in private.

I have confidence in my people that with proper training they can do the work. I delegate responsibilities.

I have worked to create an atmosphere where people can laugh at mistakes.

12. I have not been totally genuine with my people at times. (Chs. 6, 7, 9)

13. Sometimes my discipline meetings are vague or sometimes I avoid responsibilities as a manager who needs to keep people on track. (Ch. 7)

14. I tend to feel that I am not the most optimistic person in my department. (Chs. 5, 8)

15. I play favorites or make special exceptions for certain people. (Chs. 3, 6, 7)

16. I am not a good model for my people. (Chs. 4, 5, 9)

17. I criticize my employees in front of each other. (Chs. 3, 7)

18. I take on too much, including what should be their responsibilities. (Chs. 4, 6, 10)

19. I lack humor in the office. (Chs. 4, 5, 8)

A Leader's Checklist of Strategies to Encourage

Tends to discourage	Neither discouraging nor encouraging	Tends to encourage
20. I tend to keep the things I know to myself. (Chs. 4, 9, 10)		Everything (except confidential material) that I know I am willing to share with my people.
21. I feel that I do too much nit-picking and flaw finding. (Chs. 4, 5, 6)		I am more like a talent scout and have an ability to see hidden assets and resources in my people.
22. I probably take too much credit that could be given to them. (Chs. 5, 9)		I am constantly trying to give credit where credit is due.
23. I just don't give my people enough of my time. (Chs. 3, 9)		My people know and really feel that I have an open door for them when they need it.
24. I tend to use intimidation or pulling rank to motivate my people. (Chs. 3, 4, 9)		I tend to use encouragement to motivate my people.
25. I emphasize competition among my people. (Ch. 10)		I focus on mutual cooperation as opposed to competition to build team power.

26. I recognize only jobs well done. (Chs. 3, 10)

I give recognition for effort and improvement, not only the finished task.

27. I blow up or explode at mistakes. (Chs. 3, 4, 9, 10)

I can deal with things rationally and get the ship back on course.

28. I feel that I am different from my people and am more important than them. (Chs. 3, 5, 6, 9)

I am a team player and everyone has his or her responsibilities.

Ten Crucial Things to Remember and Ten Practical Things to Do from Chapter 1

1. **Remember:** Your leadership style makes the difference in the team's attitude, pride, productivity, trust, involvement, creativity, synergy, morale, and creativity, so...

    Do: Make a commitment to become an even more encouraging leader by developing and using the skills and attitudes identified as being present in encouraging leaders.

2. **Remember:** The encouraging leader is not a deep-rooted psychological concept or a mystical theory but is, very simply, a person who presents a "way of being" that tends to lead to a more harmonious and productive relationship with teammates, so...

    Do: Ask yourself the following questions that lead to some practical, applicable leadership answers: (1) What were some of the characteristics of encouraging leaders I met? (2) How can I develop some of those characteristics with my team today?

3. **Remember:** Discouraging leaders tend to talk too much, while encouraging leaders spend more time listening in order to understand their team members, so...

    Do: Meet with your most discouraged person and really listen to his or her perspective. Then develop an encouragement plan based upon what you heard. Refer to Chapter 3 for positive communication approaches.

4. **Remember:** Discouraging leaders were identified as those who focused on what was wrong rather than what was right with their team members, so...

    Do: Take some time to identify the strengths, assets, and resources of your team. Point out what has been done right. See Chapter 4 on approaches to building teammates.

5. **Remember:** Discouraging leaders rarely show team members why their roles are necessary and what contribution they provide to the team or the world, so...
   Do: Give your team's work meaning and purpose beyond the paycheck. Show team members how their work is significant. Refer to Chapter 5 for ways to instill job significance.

6. **Remember:** Discouraging leaders disrespect team members and believe they are incapable, while encouraging leaders respect the team by constantly communicating, "I believe in you. We can do it!" so...
   Do: Convey positive expectations in a discouraged person by giving him or her a job you ordinary might not and communicate your belief in that person. See Chapter 6 for ideas on how to create a winning feeling on the team.

7. **Remember:** Discouraging leaders often use public embarrassment, sarcasm, or cynicism to deal with difficult people, while encouraging leaders steer the discouraged person back onto the constructive path, so...
   Do: Memorize and use the Ten-Step Process of Assertive Encouragement listed in Chapter 7 if you need to discipline.

8. **Remember:** Discouraging leaders make excuses, blame others, or retreat into pessimism during tough times, while encouraging leaders face crises head on and are motivated by the conviction that all problems have solutions, so...
   Do: Be the leader if your team is facing a crisis to rise above the problem and mobilize your unlimited creative resources. See Chapter 8 for approaches to help your team find a way.

9. **Remember:** Discouraging leaders lack inner security and have to use their position to fill their ego or

power needs, while encouraging leaders are more interested in getting the job done than looking good because they are secure within themselves, so...

Do: Give credit to the team, rather than taking it yourself. Refer to Chapter 9 for ideas on improving morale and involvement.

10. **Remember:** Discouraging leaders tend to play team members against each other by emphasizing competition over cooperation, while encouraging leaders highlight the necessity for cooperation to build team power, so...

   Do: Think "we," "our," and "us." See Chapter 10 for team-building strategies.

Now begin your encouraging leadership development program by understanding the five insights into human behavior.

2

FIVE INSIGHTS TO MAKE YOU A MOTIVATING TEAM LEADER

Motivating team leaders have a powerful ally. They have no less than human nature on their side.

It's Only Human Nature to Want to Grow (Actualize)

The most natural behavior in the world is the infant's high level of motivation to explore—at nature's pace—his or her world. The infant doesn't panic after making a mistake, but simply looks to correct it. However, when the infant experiences criticisms of his or her imperfect tries, feelings of personal inadequacies in the superior world outside develop. Anticipation of possible mistakes activates the little one to be cautious. The original natural motivation and courage to create and explore become bridled by fear, and discouragement sets in. Years later, we see this "unmotivated" teammate afraid to try new ways of doing things, as a perfectionist with migraines, or as having a poor self-concept. But human nature started out on the infant's side.

It's Only Human Nature to Want to Contribute

It's human nature for the infant to want to contribute, to share what he or she can give. Picture a child proudly holding out his or her drawing or picking a flower to give to mom or dad. While lecturing at a university in Vancouver, B.C., I asked about 500 people to draw a picture of a horse and requested a few volunteers to share their drawings with the group. I had only two takers, a four-year-old girl and a five-year-old boy—the two children in the audience! Why were there no adult volunteers? The child's desire to contribute becomes blocked when he or she runs into know-it-alls, critics, and perfectionists. In the organization, we see this "unmotivated" individual as someone who never gives anything extra or never wants to contribute. But human nature did not originally design this being that way.

It's Only Human Nature to Want to Belong

It's human nature for the infant to want to belong to a social unit. Teams are a natural, necessary part of a person's life. The loneliest words of a child or an adult are "I wasn't included." Children enjoy being picked up and proudly explain to strangers where they fit in as they proclaim, "That's my daddy." Only after they experience conditional belonging (we accept you only if you act this or that way) do they see themselves as only belonging when they act in certain ways. On the team, this is seen in the outsider, the rebel, or the person who resists cooperation.

It's Only Human Nature to Be Open to Explore New Ideas

It's only human nature for the infant to be open, honest, genuine, and vulnerable. This golden realness starts to bronze upon hearing warnings issued about life. "Don't talk to those people," "It's a dog eat dog world," or "You can't trust them" are just a few of the many insights that create the callousness we see in some adults. On the team, we recognize this person as close-minded, distrusting, cold, and distant. However, this person wasn't born that way.

The infant has a high level of motivation to grow, to explore, to contribute, to belong, and to be open, honest, genuine, real, and vulnerable. Sometimes life's experiences can be discouraging, but an encouraging leader—with the help of human nature—can remove the chains that block natural motivation and help people find fulfillment on the team.

In order to encourage, the leader needs a model or a map of what makes people tick. The map used in this book was first drawn by Alfred Adler and was later detailed by his pupil Rudolf Dreikurs. Adler's map was selected because it has two important qualities. First, this encouraging map offers a practical guide to understanding discouragement and the encouragement process and offers workable ideas. Second, Adler's blueprint for human motivation was selected because it is positive and hopeful. The emphasis on positive approaches over negative approaches is obvious when we recall from Chapter 1 the list of leadership behaviors that were most effective in encouraging. They tended to be positive approaches to people. This map of understanding human behavior has five major insights, many outlined by Adler and a few added from *Turning People On* (L. Losoncy, 1977).

Five Human Behavior Insights of the Encouraging Leader

Encouraging Insight #1

People act out of the way they (not I) look at life. To motivate them, I have to spend some time understanding their "private logic."

The four-year-old boy with a tykish curiosity on his face nudges his mother as he looks up at her and asks the simple question, "Mommy, where's daddy?" Mother looks down and casually responds, "Honey, your father is tied up at the office." Envisioning his poor daddy gagging and in ropes on the office floor and his mother so unconcerned, the little boy panics.

He acts out of the way he (not his mother) looks at life. The philosophy of phenomenology argues that our behaviors stem from our view of the situation, not the "facts" of the situation. The facts are that the little boy's father is okay. His panic is a result of his subjective view.

Epictetus, the stoic philosopher, concluded, "Men are not disturbed by things, only thinking makes them disturbed." Indeed, Adler argued that "if a person believes he or she was just bitten by a snake it matters not whether the bite actually took place from a strictly psychological perspective." This person's behavior will be determined by that view. To take another example, it is insignificant whether or not someone is really "out to get" the paranoid person. The person's behavior will be dictated by the view that "someone is after me." He or she will be afraid of what amounts to, in fact, no one. An encouraging leader starts with the other person's phenomenological view, the "private logic."

One member of a church never volunteered to help at the fund-raising bazaars. The pastor was concerned, especially since some parishioners felt she was taking advantage of everyone else's work. The church leader decided to talk with the reluctant parishioner. It turned out that the suggestions the so-called lazy lady had made at a meeting about how to improve the bazaar were flatly rejected.

She apologetically shared, "I felt put down and stupid, and that I really had nothing to offer anyway. I thought that they'd be happy if I didn't get in the way." The leader shared this with the group (with the woman's permission), and the following year she was selected to be a contributing member of the baked goods committee—all because the leader took the time to understand the "private logic" of his church citizen. She acted out of the way that she (not the congregation) looked at things.

The simplest and at the same time one of the most incomprehensible rules of human behavior is that all behavior makes sense when we view it from the actor's perspective; the four-year-old who panicked at his daddy being tied up and the uninvolved church member's lack of involvement made total sense when we saw the situation from their view. And so does the rebel, the change resister, the chronic absentee, the alcoholic, and even the suicidal person's behavior make sense when we explore their "private logic" and their limited vantage point. The behavior may not make sense to the observer, who has a different "private logic," but it makes sense to the actor.

With this awareness of insight #1 (people act out of the way they, not I, look at life), what would an encouraging leader do that someone lacking the insight would not? Consider the following two directions that a leader could take with a person who is slowly becoming unmotivated. One way is to move away from understanding the person's private logic and the other is to move toward understanding the person's private logic.

The discouraging leader	*The encouraging leader*
Moving away from the actor's logic or imposing one's own logic on the person.	Moving toward understanding the private logic of the other person.

The discouraging leader	*The encouraging leader*
"You'll just never get anywhere in the organization if you keep associating with those negative people and listening to their ideas."	"Your friends and I often disagree about things. And I'd really be interested in better understanding what they feel is wrong here. Their suggestions and yours could be helpful in making the organization grow. But it will be helpful only if we can talk. Can you share some of your thoughts with me?"

Which would be a more effective leadership approach—the one that moves away, ignores, or squelches a different private logic or the one that moves toward understanding the joining of two private logics to form a "common sense?"

It is important to keep in mind that moving toward another person's private logic does not necessarily mean moving toward agreeing with his or her phenomenological world. You can truly understand someone else's world, but disagree with it from the standpoint of your own world. There will, of course, be times when the "private logic" of another begins to make sense to you. What a benefit to gain! An increased insight is yours because of your willingness to understand.

Every day provides free opportunities to sharpen your leadership skills by mastering the first insight of encouragement: People act out of the way they (not I) look at life. Try it with someone with whom you totally disagree. Begin to see how that person thinks. Discovering how someone else thinks is a secret to success with others. Captain Lou Puskas, one of the top fishermen in the eastern United States, was asked why he is so successful in pulling in the big catch. He responded, "You've got to think like a fish. When it rains or when it is windy, calm, or sunny, you imagine where they would go. Then you go there."

Whether you are a fisher of men, a vice-president of a steel company, or the manager of a record shop, understanding how your people think will be the key to your success with them.

Encouraging Insight #2

People can best be understood by observing the social consequences of their actions.

The manager of a small card shop becomes furious and loses her temper after learning that her employees have been rude to some customers. She starts kicking card racks and shouting obscenities. The two employees decide to walk out on her, leaving no one else in the shop to observe her actions. How long do you think she continues kicking and throwing? Not long. Why? No audience, no show! With no one to observe, the behavior no longer has a social consequence, that is, the reactions of others.

Did you ever see a young child fall and then look around to see if anyone was there before he or she decided whether or not to cry? Did you ever hear someone at work complimented with a statement like "You look super in blue?" What did you observe about this person's future dress pattern? Were you ever told by someone you respect that you had a real talent in a particular area? Did you then highlight that asset or talent in the other person's presence? People's behavior can best be understood by being aware of their "private logic" of what other people are looking for in them.

An interesting fact about people is that the social consequences of attention and recognition are so important that many conclude, "If I can't get my attention needs taken care of by doing the right thing, I will do the *wrong* thing (discouraged)." At least the social consequences of attention are received.

Consider the following example of how misdirected

behavior to get attention was rerouted by an encouraging leader who altered the social consequences. An 18-year-old girl working at a fast-food restaurant was an extreme attention-getter in the presence of the other workers and customers and even when the manager was in the room. The manager wanted to do everything possible to help her before firing her, and she told her so, but the teenager still continued her loud behavior. In a discussion during her final warning, the manager found that the girl had an older sister who did everything perfectly, was a straight A student in school, and was accepted into a very prestigious colleges. The manager also discovered that her attention-seeking employee was always second best and never got attention from her parents, like her sister did—until she got into trouble. Then they noticed her. The insightful manager realized that she had not given much attention to the girl when she did the right thing and only recognized her when she needed disciplining. During the next three days, the manager would from time to time gave the teenager attention for working well with the other employees. She caught her in the act of "being responsible." The manager created a social setting in which the girl could get her attention needs fulfilled through constructive behavior. Her job was saved.

The encouraging leader is always aware that people's behavior can best be understood by observing the social consequences of their behavior. The leader tries to understand each person's logic in deciding "what behavior will work to get me attention." When a person's attention needs are fulfilled by positive actions, that person becomes increasingly involved and productive.

Dr. Richard Cahn, superintendent of a large northeastern U.S. school district, employs encouragement in the school organization. Cahn concludes about people:

> It has been my observation that people are more fulfilled by performing well than by performing poorly, by contributing instead of being uncoopera-

tive and by feeling recognized rather than by feeling insignificant.

People can find this fulfillment when an encouraging atmosphere exists (Dinkmeyer and Losoncy, 1995).

A discouraging leader's approach to a discouraged person	*An encouraging leader's approach to a discouraged person*
I'll wait for that irresponsible behavior to occur again and I will come down on (give my attention to) him or her.	Let me give attention today to what that person does right.
	If the discouraged behavior occurs again, I will, as best as possible, ignore it (not give attention to it). However, I must immediately give my attention when the person again acts inappropriately. Only if the disruptive actions continue will I confront (see Chapter 7).

Encouraging Insight #3

Individual uniqueness is not to be ignored, but rather is to be explored and highlighted. Uniqueness is the very source of personal energy.

In the age of technology, society has tried to organize individuals into categories so that people would fit into the finite mind of the computer. The computer, however, is limited in its ability to give a person every uniqueness that is rightfully his or hers. Whenever we attempt to "quantify" people, we disqualify their uniqueness. This is unfortunate, and, of course, new ways of viewing people to incorporate both the machine and the person at higher levels is inevitable.

That higher level incorporation of machine and person is discussed by John Naisbitt (1982) in *Megatrends*.

In describing the ten trends society is experiencing, the author states that the age of technology needs to provide high technology/high touch. Naisbitt argues that with increased technology must come increased literal and figurative touch of people to fulfill their human needs.

An encouraging leader must "touch" people in some way, and the touch must be real. How do I know if I am being touched in a genuine way? I know it if you recognize my uniqueness, the ways that belong to this special organism called "me."

The encouraging leader makes extraordinary people out of ordinary ones by taking the time to observe each person's own unique "private logic" and own unique talents and goals. The encouraging leader may be the first person ever to give someone the gift of being understood.

How a discouraging leader looks at a group	*How an encouraging leader looks at the uniqueness of each member*
You people...	Each of you has something special to offer. Think of what you can contribute in your own unique way.

Encouraging Insight #4

Unmotivated individuals are not sick, bad, lazy, or stupid. Unmotivated individuals are viewed as discouraged. The antidote to discouragement is encouragement.

How many people would not want to see faces light up when they walk into a room? How many would not want to feel like they had at least a small rippling effect on the waters of life during their lifetime? Who would rather be imprisoned by life's possibilities than fully living them? Very few.

Encouraging leaders have human nature on their side. Discouraged people feel they can't make it, they have nothing to offer, they will make a mistake, they will be taken advantage of, they will be snubbed or laughed at, or believe that there is an "easier way" to achieve success (defined by their own private logic).

It is enlightening to see a "lazy person" move into a new setting with an encouraging leader who recognizes that person's talents, strength, and resources. The laziness somehow disappears!

It is incredible to see a "sick" person in the presence of two different psychiatrists—one who talks disease and who talks potential. The person walks out of each office differently.

It is amazing to see a "slow" student in the presence of two different teachers—one who goes with the label and one who sees the uniqueness of the discouraged youth. The difference is everything.

Encouraging Insight #5

People are viewed as being responsible for their actions.

The old debate that centered on the issue of what causes human behavior—heredity or environment—seems to be leading to the conclusion that neither is the ultimate influence. A reading of Marilyn Ferguson's extensive work entitled *The Aquarian Conspiracy* provides strong support for a third cause. This newer, more optimistic perspective of what makes people tick argues for the power of self-determination. Adler and many others observed many people who transcended environments devoid of golden spoons to achieve greatness. Adler argued:

> Do not forget the most important fact that not heredity and not environment are determining factors. Both are giving only the frame and the influence which are answered by the individual in regard to his styled, creative power (Ansbacher and Ansbacher, 1956).

David Schwartz, in his powerful offering entitled *The Magic of Getting What You Want,* provides some valuable insights into the rewards of self-determinism:

Huge, prosperous businesses such as McDonald's, Ford, Kentucky Fried Chicken and Amway were started by people with very little capital. Furthermore, Presidents Coolidge, Hoover, Truman, Eisenhower, Johnson, Nixon, Ford, Carter, and Reagan—all except two of the people who led the nation in modern times— were born to poor or modestly well-off parents. Presidents Roosevelt and Kennedy were the only exceptions (Schwartz, 1983).

There are two major approaches leaders can take toward their people: passive and active. In the passive position, the leader sees his or her people with limited capabilities based on factors such as environment, circumstances, luck, intelligence, or education. Taking the passive posture often means spending energies digging up the "excuse," the "blame," or the reason for the limitation.

Describing the passive view, Losoncy wrote in *You Can Do It*:

The unproductive way of understanding the causes for your feelings, thoughts, and actions is to conclude they were caused by someone or something other than yourself. At least four different types of blame receivers can be distinguished. These four are group blame (the other school is much bigger than ours so they'll beat us), other person blame (e.g., my teachers didn't explain things well), thing blame (e.g., this cloudy weather makes me lazy) and self-blame (e.g., I'm not the kind of person who was built to be a leader) (L. Losoncy, 1980).

Passive leaders wait for circumstances to change, for the right moment to arrive. But waiting for the world to change before we change is like looking at our reflection in a mirror and saying, "You move first."

Active self-starting leaders take responsibility to make things happen. They take any circumstance, no matter how challenging, and say, "It's up to me to mobilize my people resources and find a solution to the problem."

Let's contrast the attitudes of two leaders, one passive and one active, and decide which one you would want on your team.

Passive leader's outlook	*Active leader's outlook*
1. What's the use! I can't control the economy. Only money motivates people, so I'll just have to wait until the economy shifts and my people get their raises before I can expect to see motivated employees.	1. The major reason why most of my employees work is financial, and right now the economy is bad. Unfortunately, I can't control the world's economy, but, as a leader, I can control many other factors that contribute to productivity, such as pride in achievement, recognition for skills and talents, understanding of employee frustration, etc. Let me develop an employee motivation strategy.
2. These kids just aren't motivated. There's nothing I can do about it. It's the schools, permissive child-rearing practices, increased drug use, and so on that causes it. No, there's nothing I can do about the fact that kids nowadays don't want to work.	2. These kids today are an exciting challenge for a manager because some of them are not motivated in the same ways we managers are. Like a detective, I'll spend time finding clues to solve the problem of motivating the young workers of today. By developing different strategies, I will enhance my skills in motivating an important segment of the work force. Every day of work is a free opportunity for me to understand how to motivate young people. Every day provides a greater opportunity than taking all the college courses in the world on motivating people.

Passive leader's outlook	*Active leader's outlook*
3. We tried selling the Smith account before. They are just too stubborn. Don't waste your time!	3. The Smith account is a big one. We want it. The approaches we used before didn't work. Let's brainstorm and find a way!

Which leader is more likely to get things done? Obviously, the one who tries, the one who believes that "It's up to us to take responsibility and find a solution to the challenge" will see better results.

Encouraging leaders have respect for the abilities of responsible self-starters. They always do better, and their belief in people motivates their people to soar higher.

Five Insights to Make You a Motivating Leader

People are attracted to the positive energies of a motivating leader. They want a reason to go on, and they want to contribute, belong, and be open and genuine. Human nature is on the side of the motivating leader.

Many unmotivated or irresponsible people are simply discouraged. To encourage, a leader needs a map of what makes people tick in order to understand why they act the way they do.

In this chapter, five insights about people were discussed in order to better understand them:

- **Encouraging insight #1:** People act out of the way they (not I) look at life. To motivate them, I have to spend some time trying to understand each person's private logic.

- **Encouraging insight #2:** People can best be understood by observing the social consequences of their actions.

- **Encouraging insight #3:** Individual uniqueness is not

to be ignored, but rather explored, even highlighted. Uniqueness is the very source of personal energy.

- **Encouraging insight #4:** Unmotivated individuals are not sick, bad, lazy, or stupid. Unmotivated people are discouraged. The antidote to discouragement is encouragement

- **Encouraging insight #5:** People are viewed as being responsible for their actions.

Ten Things to Remember and Ten Practical Things to Do from Chapter 2

1. **Remember:** People operate out of the way they look at life, so...
    Do: Take time to look at the world from the perspective of the discouraged teammate to sense his or her private logic. You then will be in a much better position to motivate.

2. **Remember:** All behavior makes sense when we view it from the actor's perspective, so...
    Do: Instead of condemning another's actions, first understand that the behavior was logical to the person at the time. Communicate that understanding, and then add a new perspective to help the person grow.

3. **Remember:** People can best be understood by observing the social consequences of their actions, so...
    Do: Remember that discouraged, unmotivated, irresponsible people need to receive different social consequences from you, the leader. Don't give attention for negative behavior, but instead recognize positive behavior.

4. **Remember:** Contrary to popular opinion in the past, it is now recognized that, for the good of the whole

team, emphasizing competition hurts more than it helps, so...
Do: Carefully assess your everyday style to eliminate any attitudes that might convey that you are playing one person against another. (See Chapter 10 for further details.)

5. **Remember:** Your unproductive, unmotivated, or uninvolved team members are discouraged and may be telling you that they feel as though they don't belong or that their contribution is insignificant, so...
Do: Make a plan to help your discouraged person feel like a part of the team (see Chapter 10) and feel that the work he or she does each day has meaning (see Chapter 5).

6. **Remember:** A few of your unmotivated people may feel lost, alienated, or lost among the group, so...
Do: If you sense that a team member has developed the feeling that "I am just a number, not a person," become determined to devote a few extra minutes to fire up his or her feelings of uniqueness.

7. **Remember:** Most people are more fulfilled by performing well than by performing poorly, by contributing than by being uncooperative, and by feeling recognized than by feeling insignificant. People can find this fulfillment in an encouraging atmosphere, so...
Do: With this attitude in mind, proceed to develop the skills, strategies, and attitudes that encouraging leaders have.

8. **Remember:** Individual uniqueness is not to be ignored, but rather explored and highlighted, so...
Do: Identify unique skills, talents, strengths, and resources in each of your people—and tell them!

9. **Remember:** Unmotivated individuals are not viewed as sick, bad, lazy, or stupid. They are discouraged, so...

> **Do:** The remedy to discouragement is not blaming, diagnosing, or name–calling. The remedy to discouragement is your encouragement.

10. **Remember:** Active leaders believe that people can act responsibly to solve problems, so...
    Do: Communicate to your people that you believe. Instead of looking for excuses together, look for answers together.

Now it's time to explore the skills development program presented in this book. Keep in mind the power present in the "way of being" of the leader and the five insights about people. Techniques that you can use today to bring about better communication, greater harmony, and mutual respect in your unit are addressed in Chapter 3.

3

Positive Leadership Approaches to Resolve Team Differences

Ironically, the leader is the most dependent people on the team. The higher one's position, the more people a person needs to hold him or her up. Leaders are dependent upon those whom they lead. The leader's success is based on the performance of those he or she leads. When the team-mates are motivated to work together to achieve the team's goals, the leader becomes successful. However, when the members of the team are immersed in conflict, miscom-munication, or misunderstanding, a different type of motivation exists—negative motivation. Negative motiva-tion is seen in a selfish, narrow-minded desire to prove someone wrong and a feeling of personal martyrdom. These misdirected motivations waste energies that could be used constructively instead of in destructive directions. Both the team and the leader lose.

By default, the leader is the most likely candidate to take the responsibility for initiating plans to resolve the differences among people. The leader has the most to lose. Differences result from what in Chapter 2 was re-ferred to as the "private logic" held by each member.

Leadership's task is to bring together the private logic of many to form a common sense.

Even the most highly motivated leader is cognizant of the fact that resolving differences of private logic is no easy task. The job is especially formidable when you consider the natural disagreements that tend to occur. The private logic of the commissioned salesperson is often different from the private logic of the collection department. The private logic of the waitress (who faces the public and hears their complaints about the food) is almost always different from the private logic of the chef who cooked the food. The private logic of the beauty salon owner who invests thousands of dollars to start the business is often different from the private logic of the haircutter who wonders why she only gets fifty percent and the owner gets fifty percent. The private logic of the high school football coach is different from the private logic of the parents of the player sitting on the bench.

In larger the organizations, the private logic of individuals snowballs into a "limited group logic" that makes the issue even more complex. One of the most interesting experiences I ever had was serving as a consultant to a Pennsylvania school district. In this capacity, I had the opportunity to work with school board members, school administrators, teachers, custodians, students, and parents. I worked with each group on "How to Be Encouraging" and "How to Communicate More Effectively." The length of the sessions varied from three to thirty hours with each group.

What insights I gained! Every, yes *every*, group in the organization had something in common. Each thought that it was getting a raw deal in the organization. The board members, for example, felt that they were unpaid scapegoats and were basically unappreciated. The school administrators felt that their hands were tied and that they couldn't make any decisions without rocking the boat. If they did, the ax would come down on them. The teachers blamed the school board for not caring, the administrators for not disciplining the students, and the children for not listening. The secondary school teachers even blamed the elementary school teachers for not preparing the children for high school. In turn, the elementary school teachers blamed the parents for permissive child-rearing practices. The custodians criticized the administrators for not laying down the law on keeping the cafeteria and hallways clean. The janitors blamed the teachers and students for not "picking up" after themselves in the classrooms. The students blamed the administrators for tough, inflexible rules and accused many teachers of not caring and of being interested only in getting their paychecks. The parents blamed the school board members for using their position as a steppingstone to gain political clout, blamed the administrators for punishing their children when the teachers were at fault, and blamed the teachers for not teaching!

In other experiences, I found similar misunderstandings to exist in most organizations. Unfortunately, the energy that is diverted to build stronger arguments in support of one's own private logic or the limited group logic is energy that could be used to achieve common team goals.

Approaches to building understanding, mutual respect, and open communication among your people are presented in this chapter. If your unit is faced with any of the following problems, this chapter has relevance:

1. Social cliques
2. Interdepartmental conflicts
3. Scapegoats
4. Unappreciated people
5. Stubbornness
6. Poor morale
7. Lack of communication
8. Disrespect

9.   Misunderstandings

10. Egoism

Six approaches to resolving people problems are discussed:

- Transferring
- Undiagnosing
- Peeking
- De-escalating
- Exposing
- Linking

Approach #1: Transferring

Transferring involves encouraging people to "transfer" from their own world and walk a mile in their teammate's shoes to understand the other person's own unique responsibilities, pressures, frustrations, and conflicts.

Transferring is a leadership approach taken to minimize jealousies, narrow-mindedness, misunderstandings, and differences based on differing responsibilities. Transferring is most appropriately used when some sort of disharmony exists among people or departments. It is an attempt to broaden the private logic of the parties and to create a common sense. Transferring is based on Encouraging Insight #1 from Chapter 2: People operate out of the way they (not I) look at life. To motivate them, I have to spend some time trying to understand their private logic.

The charismatic vice-president of human resources is continually confronted by the vice-president of finance about the irresponsible sales department. The accounting executive typically explodes, "Our psychopathic sales force promises everything and wants to give away the world to the customer. All you have to do to be a salesperson is be a sharp-talking worm brain. They have no responsibilities other than making a sale at any cost, and then we in finance face the burden of accounting for the monies in the end."

The human resource specialist is intrigued because he is continually bombarded by the vice-president of sales, who reflects frustration over the money man always on his back.

Is there an answer? Yes—transferring. The vice-president of human resources urged each leader to take three days and get into the work world of the other—to transfer himself to the other's world and see what life looks like. Both were encouraged to open their minds, feel the unique pressures and frustrations of the "other side," and then communicate to develop a practical plan to work together.

The vice-president of finance made the following report to his people a month later:

> The pressures on our salespeople here are different than the pressures on us. First, they feel the responsibility from the whole company to produce, produce, produce. And it's tough during these times. Second, they get to know the customer intimately, and sometimes they make promises based on their personal relationship. In accounting, perhaps the customer is viewed more as an account, maybe more objectively, and we have trouble understanding the pressures of that specific account. Third, the salesperson's living and, in fact, retention of his or her job is based simply on sales. Our jobs aren't. I guess if I were in sales, maybe some of my attitudes about salespeople would change and would be more in harmony with their views. I have tried to understand their world and they have tried to understand our pressures. Together we are developing a plan to make life easier for everyone.

Transferring involves encouraging people to spend some time in the world of the responsibilities of other people. For example, the grill person at a fast-food restaurant should work up front for a day and the order taker should work behind the grill.

How can you, as a leader, use transferring to help your team?

Approach #2: Undiagnosing

Undiagnosing is the process of trying to understand rather than "diagnose," label, or judge a teammate.

Sometimes leaders are able to put their fingers on a problem, diagnose it, and even label the problem, but have no practical course of action to follow to motivate. The diagnosis didn't work, so the next logical course of action is to—undiagnose.

Ben is a troubled employee, and everyone on the team knows he has a drinking problem. While it interferes with his performance only slightly, the potential for poor quality work exists in the future. Ben's manager, Ed, has labeled Ben an alcoholic, a view that is generally supported by the personnel department. The well-intentioned manager has even suggested that Ben seek help, but Ben keeps resisting, saying that everything will be okay.

Ed realizes that labeling Ben an alcoholic does nothing in itself to help Ben unless he is motivated to seek assistance. With a strong desire to help the discouraged person, Ed decides to do something that might be more practical.

First, Ed forgot about the label of alcoholic (undiagnose). Next, he transferred to Ben's world to see how the situation looks from Ben's private logic (see Chapter 2). While sitting in his office one day, he takes a few minutes to make a mental visit to Ben's world.

Diagnosing	*Undiagnosing and transferring*
CONCLUSION: Ben is an alcoholic.	CONCLUSION: "My life is a mess. My wife left me and took my daughter with her. And it's all my fault. On top of that, I'm dead-ended in my job, with no possible promotion. My work is terribly routine, boring, and gives me no satisfaction. I've gained so much weight recently that it's uncomfortable for me to even walk. I've lost respect for myself. Life seems to be hopeless, and I'm digging myself into a deeper and deeper rut. Nothing seems to matter anymore. The only time I feel good about things is when I get away and get a few belts of whiskey. The bartender and the guys at the club understand me. They remember my high school touchdown."

After experiencing the transfer, Ed is in a much better position to understand and connect with Ben's world. By accurately understanding Ben, Ed was able to apply some of the strategies of encouragement. He decided that in a small way he would provide some of that valuable social attention that the bartender gave to Ben. He started asking Ben about his sports experiences and was able to apply some of the assets involved in being a football player on a team to Ben's role at work. According to Ed, "Ben's face lit up."

Diagnosing	*Undiagnosing and transferring*
TREATMENT: Recommend he seek help.	TREATMENT: 1. Share with Ben his assets that you admire. 2. Discuss with him his feelings about alternate future possibilities.

Diagnosing	Undiagnosing and transferring
	3. Convey an understanding of the difficulties that he must be experiencing at this time.
	4. Convey hope and open the door to future communication.
BEN'S RESPONSE: No.	BEN'S RESPONSE: Feelings of importance and acceptance, more willing to communicate. This increased willingness to talk with someone who respects him enhances the chance of his accepting advice.

Undiagnosing is the process of unlabeling someone (lazy, paranoid, etc.) after discovering that the label gives no practical help. Transferring to the other person's world to see what it looks like involves spotting the needs, pressures, and frustrations and moving to remedy the problem.

How could you use undiagnosing to be a more effective leader in your organization?

_____

_____

_____

Approach #3: Peeking

Peeking is looking under a teammate's surface behaviors, feelings, and beliefs to "peek" at the true underlying motivations.

Peeking is an approach that many motivating leaders use quite naturally. Yet the same ideas are available to any sensitive person who wants to peek beyond the surface of someone's actions or feelings and see the real person. Peeking is consistent with psychiatrist Carl Jung's concept that what we see in people is often their mask and not the real self. Jung argued that the mask may even be the exact opposite of the real underlying self. The following poem expresses the difference between the real and underlying selves and points to the importance of peeking at discouraged people:

Please Hear What I Am Not Saying

Don't be fooled by me
Don't be fooled by the face I wear.
    For I wear a mask. I wear a thousand masks.
    Masks that I'm afraid to take off.
    And none of them are me.
Pretending is an art that's second nature with me,
    But don't be fooled,
    For god's sake don't be fooled.
I give you the impression that I'm secure.
    That all is sunny and unruffled with me,
    Within as well as without.
    That confidence is my name and coolness my game,
    That water's calm and I'm in command,
    And that I need no one.
But don't believe me,
Please,
My surface may seem smooth, but my surface is my mask,
    My ever-varying and ever-concealing mask.
    Beneath lies no smugness, no complacence.
    Beneath dwells the real me in confusion, in fear,
    In aloneness.
But I hide this.
I don't want anybody to know it.
I panic at the thought of my weakness and fear being exposed.
That's why I frantically create a mask to hide behind.
    A nonchalant, sophisticated facade, to help me pretend
    To shield me from the glance that knows.
But such a glance is precisely my salvation,

My salvation, and I know it.
That is, if it's followed by acceptance.
If it's followed by love.
It's the only thing that can liberate me from myself,
    From my own self-built prison walls,
        From the barriers that I so painstakingly erect.
It's the only thing that will assure me of what I cannot
    assure myself,
        That I am really worth something.
But I don't tell you this, I don't dare.
I'm afraid to.
I'm afraid your glance will not be followed by
    acceptance and love.
I'm afraid that deep down I'm nothing.
    That I'm no good,
    And that you will see this and reject me.
So I play my game,
    My desperate pretending game,
    With a facade of masks,
    That glittering but empty parades of masks.
    And my life becomes a front.
I idly chatter to you in the suave tones of surface talk.
I tell you everything that's really nothing,
    And nothing of what's everything,
    Of what's crying within me.
So when I'm through my routine—
    Don't be fooled by what I'm saying.
Please listen carefully, and hear what I'm Not saying.
    What I'd like to be able to say,
    What for survival I need to say,
    But what I can't say.
I dislike hiding.
Honestly.
I dislike the superficial game I'm playing.
    The superficial, phony game.
I really like to be genuine and spontaneous,
    And me, but you've got to help me.
You've got to hold out your hand,
    Even when that's the last thing I seem to want,
        or need.

Only you can wipe away from my eyes the blank stare
    of the breathing dead.
        Only you can call me into aliveness.
Each time you're kind, and gentle, and encouraging,
        Each time you try to understand because you
            really care,
        My heart begins to grow wings, very small wings,
        Very feeble wings.
        But wings.
With your sensitivity and sympathy
        And your power of understanding,
        You can breathe life into me.
I want you to know that.
I want you to know how important you are to me.
        How you can be a creator of the person that is me,
        If you choose to,
        Please choose to.
You alone can break down the wall behind which I
    tremble,
You alone can remove my mask,
You alone can release me from my shadow-world of
    panic and uncertainty,
        From my lonely prison.
So do not pass me by.
Please do not pass me by.
It will not be easy for you,
A long conviction of worthlessness builds strong walls.
The nearer you approach to me, the blinder I may
    strike back.
It's irrational, but despite what the books say about man,
        I am irrational.
I fight against the very thing I cry out for.
But I am told that love is stronger than strong walls,
        And in this lies my hope.
My only hope.
Please try to beat down those walls with firm hands.
        But with gentle hands.
Who am I, you may wonder?
I am someone you know very well.
For I am every man and woman you meet.

                                    Anonymous

Jack and Judy sell household products in their family business and work closely with a few hundred other families who have done the same. The husband and wife are known for their sensitivity. For example, they always remember company anniversaries and do something nice for their people. On one occasion, they forgot an important anniversary, and the couple, John and Sally Harris, became upset. John Harris angrily asserted, "You know, we've been with you much longer than most, and others—even on their first anniversary—are honored."

Judy, a sensitive lady, saw Mr. Harris's surface emotion of anger. But she didn't respond to the anger; instead, she peeked at the real underlying feeling—hurt.

"John, what a horrible oversight on our part. I'm sure it must have hurt you and Sally, especially after you worked so hard this year. I guess at times Jack and I get caught up in our work and we make mistakes. We hope that our oversight isn't viewed as a lack of caring or respect, but simply an oversight. It won't happen again."

Imagine how different the outcome would have been if Judy had responded to the surface emotion of anger rather than hurt!

Peeking is looking beyond any emotion or behavior to ask what might really be at the root and then responding to the underlying emotion. For example:

- Could anger really be hurt?

- Could acting overconfident be lack of confidence?

- Could acting disinterested be afraid of getting involved?

- Could "I'm happy just the way things are now" be "I'm afraid of taking a risk and failing"?

- Could "I hate you" be "I love you"?

- Could "I don't care" be "I care too much and it hurts, so I must numb myself"?

- Could sarcasm be the hard crust on a very sensitive person?

- Could "no soliciting" mean "If you get to me I know I'll buy, so I need signs to keep you away"?

- Could "I'm busy tonight" mean "I'm not, but I can't let you know that I have nothing to do"?

Identify some ways you could use peeking to become a more sensitive and effective leader in your organization.

_____

_____

_____

Approach #4: De-escalating

De-escalating is a communication tool that resists the natural tendency to judge a teammate as he or she speaks, which escalates the conflict into a win–lose struggle, and instead "de-escalate" by listening in order to understand the other person's feelings about the issue.

De-escalation is a concept based on the writings and ideas of Carl R. Rogers, the psychologist who in the 1960s shook the world with insights that have now become standard in effective communication. Rogers argues that there are two major ways of taking in the words of another person. One way is to *judge,* and the other way is to make every attempt to *understand* the feelings behind the words. In *On Becoming a Person,* Rogers wrote:

> ...the major barrier to mutual interpersonal communication is our very natural tendency to judge, to evaluate, to approve or disapprove the statements of the other person or group...Although the tendency to make evaluations is common in almost all interchanges of language, it is very much heightened in those situation where feelings and emotions are deeply involved...So the stronger our feelings, the more likely it is that there will be no mutual element in

communication...This tendency to react to any emotional, meaningful statement and form an evaluation
of it from our own point of view is, I repeat, the major
barrier to interpersonal communication.

But is there any way of solving this problem, of
avoiding this barrier? Real communication occurs and
this evaluative tendency is avoided when we listen
with understanding. What does this mean? It means
to see the expressed idea and attitude from the other
person's point of view, to sense how it feels to him,
to achieve his frame of reference in regard to the
thing he is talking about (Rogers, 1961).

The distance between people is not measured in feet
but in minds. People skilled in communicating with ani-
mals know that the way to invite them to move closer is
by using understanding, nonthreatening, smooth move-
ments. The motivating leader de-escalates the angry team,
family, or business member by understanding. De-escalation involves turning words into feelings instead of prov-
ing someone wrong or guilty.

When facing situations of possible escalation of conflicts, remember the following two paths:

Escalating	*De-escalating*
1. Judge: "You're right or you're wrong based on my perspective."	1. Try to understand: "I'll look at your perspective."
	2. Communicate understanding by turning words into feelings.
	3. Ask for feedback: "Do I understand correctly?"
	4. Move toward conflict resolution by asking for the same understanding in return.

De-escalating is a leadership approach that is used
to address an emotional crisis. Understand the feelings of
the other person and temporarily throw away the gavel.

How could you use de-escalating as a leader in your organization?

_____

_____

_____

Approach #5: Exposing

Exposing occurs when the leader shares his or her pressures, demands, and needs with the team members, thus "exposing" the team to the leader's vantage point.

The goal of exposing is to help people see the situation from a new or different perspective. The "law of myopia" suggests that people are more fully aware of the pressures that they themselves face than they are of the pressures faced by people on different levels. Therefore, exposing is a natural eye-opener. Some of the myopia can be removed by exposing the members to new perspectives. Knowledge is almost always better than lack of it.

Despite the powerful effects that exposing can have, many leaders resist it out of fear. There are two reasons why leaders keep information which could be understood by all to themselves: "What if they get to know as much as I know?" and "Will they recognize my flaws if they see more of the picture?" These leaders fail to realize that the more people know about the total picture, the more empathetic and helpful they are likely to become, as the following example illustrates.

The owner of a skin care salon has employees who are disgruntled over their earnings. They argue that it is unfair that they, who do most of the work, make only fifty percent commission, while the owner takes the other fifty percent from the total service dollars. In fact, one of the skin care technicians is on the verge of quitting and hopes to open up her own salon and keep the full 100 percent.

The owner doesn't know where to turn because her accountant has told her that it will be impossible to raise the employees' commission and continue to make a nine percent profit. On the other hand, the owner doesn't want to lose the employees she personally trained—along with their clientele.

The frustrated owner attends a small business management seminar and voices her dilemma. The consultant responds, "Have you shared with your people the bottom-line facts of your business?" "Of course not," the owner replies, "that's really none of their business." The consultant answers, "But, you see, the more fully aware they are about the real facts, the more likely they are to understand your situation. Without full awareness, they will naturally tip the scales of justice in their favor. The more exposure they have to the total picture, the more likely a fair settlement through understanding can take place."

The open-minded owner decides to use the exposure approach to enlighten her employees and share with them the fact that she invested thousands of dollars to open up the salon. She also points out that if she had put this money into certificates of deposit (for a ten percent return at the time), her earnings would have been more than the bottom-line nine percent profit she now makes. When the owner explained the financial picture of the business, including her costs for salary, insurance, rent, heat, telephone, supplies, electricity, maintenance, and so on, the technicians' eyes were opened to a new way of looking at the total picture. Exposing made the difference.

Exposing is the inward reversal of the transferring approach. What a combination of ways to bring about mutual understanding by exposing the facts and figures and your pressure points to the membership!

What are some ways in which you could use the approach of exposing as a leader?

Approach #6: Linking

Linking is the process whereby the leader points out similarities among the teammates to "link" them closer together in common bonds.

Some researchers argue that more people leave their jobs because of social factors than because of inability to handle the work. Clearly, many people leave organizations because of feelings of not belonging to the group. Anyone who has ever been in a group in which they felt they had little in common with the other members knows the discomfort of the feeling of being on stage alone.

Linking is the process whereby a leader identifies similarities among the membership to help everyone feel linked. Linking grew out of the social-psychological concept called "the similarity-liking effect." This effect suggests that the more familiar we are with something, the more we tend to feel comfortable with it, and the more we perceive ourselves to be similar to other people, the more we like them.

A natural xenophobia (fear of the differences in other people) exists in many people in organizations. The newcomer and the isolate are human resources that are lost because they feel like "outsiders." Outsiders are in many cases afraid to contribute and function at a safety level. Once their safety and social needs are met, they move on to fulfill higher self-esteem and self-actualization needs (Maslow, 1954). They can contribute without fear because they feel that they belong. The membership xenophobia is cured as outsiders become insiders. That process can be facilitated by linking.

Some forms of linking include:

1. **Linking with past experience.**

   "Sal, you're from Des Moines, aren't you? Did you know that Roger is from Decorah, Iowa?"

   "Well, looks like we have two Drexel University graduates here. Did you know each other before?"

2. Linking with common interests.

"I know that Tom would agree with you, Sara, that the Indians have a pennant chance, if the baseball strike ends. Tom often gets down to the stadium."

"Another movie-buff in our organization."

3. Linking with family similarities.

"You have twins also, Carol, don't you? "Ben and Joan just had twins last December."

"Did I hear you say you are going to the Marriage Encounter, Pete? Paul and Betty went last year and they had a great experience."

"Oh, yes, the 'terrible twos.' I think I know what you're going through with your little one, Jim."

4. Linking with common struggles.

"Our goal is to score this touchdown. We have two minutes. If we score, we win. We need everyone's best effort. If everyone gives their total best for two minutes, we as a team can turn this three-point deficiency around and win. That's our challenge."

"Diane, I know how it must hurt to have been turned down for that promotion. You certainly had a right to feel disappointed. The same thing happened to me a few years ago and I was devastated for about a month. Then I realized that attitude was getting me nowhere and only making me more bitter. So I put it into second gear and came back, and it was a result of that new attitude that I eventually did get this promotion. I know that now it hurts a lot, but just as the leaves grow back on the trees in the spring, there is a tomorrow."

Linking unites the divided, warms the cool, and can erase some of the uncomfortable ambiguities that we feel toward those we don't really know. By pointing out similarities, we humanize "the others," making them similar to us. We can then identify with at least a part of them, and they are part of us. We all become stronger when we are all part of the link built by the leader.

How could you use a form of linking with your people to bring about greater understanding and harmony?

_____

_____

_____

Ten Crucial Things to Remember and Ten Practical Things to Do from Chapter 3

1. **Remember:** Many leaders feel that too much of their time is spent on dealing with problems that are the result of misunderstandings and poor communication. If this is true for you, then...
   Do: Make a decision today to be a communication troubleshooter in your department. Ask yourself, "Would a little effort today save my everyday problems in the long run?" and "Is it worth my time to improve understanding and communication with my people?"

2. **Remember:** On the healthy team, people tend to be in harmony, and there exists a desire for mutual trust. The harmonious team does not happen haphazardly, but is the result of the leader's plan, so...
   Do: Assess your team to develop a sense of whether it is moving away from or toward harmony. Ask yourself the following questions: "Do I really understand my people's pressures and frustrations?" "Do they really understand the pressures and frustrations I face?" "Do my employees understand the pressures and frustrations that their co-workers face?"

3. **Remember:** The main ingredient present in encouraging leaders is their ability and willingness to listen. Empathic listening involves understanding rather than immediately judging the world of the other person, so...

   Do: Practice empathic listening today. When a teammate speaks with you, try to understand what he or she is saying from his or her perspective. Listen without judgment until the person has explained his or her position.

4. **Remember:** After you listen empathically and do an "I to you" transfer with the discouraged person, you are in an extremely strong position to motivate because you better understand that person, so...

   Do: Identify the pressures, frustrations, needs, and goals of your most discouraged person.

5. **Remember:** Relationships can be defined as being of either an "I–it" or an "I–you" nature. In I–it relationships, we tend to see other people as "its" and diagnose them. In I–you relationships, we can un-diagnose, and the other person is viewed as an individual with hopes, dreams, goals, pressures, and frustrations, so...

   Do: Experience you teammates' worlds as if you were actually them. Try transferring with the discouraged person in particular, in order to understand him or her more effectively.

6. **Remember:** Misunderstandings are often the result of the myopia that exists among people in different roles, so...

   Do: Make a plan to have people who are doing one job experience the world of people who are doing another job.

7. **Remember:** The more the members of your team feel that their teammates are similar to them, the more they will allow them inside their world, so...

Do: Link your people by identifying similarities among them.

8. **Remember:** People's actual surface behavior and emotions are often only marks of their real selves, so...
   Do: Peek beyond the surface and look for the underlying emotion instead of responding to the surface. For example, anger may, in fact, really be hurt.

9. **Remember:** Just as a hitchhiker must put a thumb to the air to indicate a need, it is important to express your needs, frustrations, pressures, and goals to your people, so...
   Do: Make sure that your people transfer to your world to experience your pressures. Expose them to your vantage point.

10. **Remember:** Your leadership style makes the difference in motivating unproductive people who are basically discouraged. Your encouragement is the antidote to discouragement, so...
    Do: Encourage by understanding the real world of your people and seek the same in return. Create an encouraging atmosphere.

4

THE MOTIVATING LEADER AS A PEOPLE BUILDER

When you observe uplifting leaders, whether they be managers, parents, coaches, or even presidents, you consistently see a common ingredient present in their philosophy of people. Motivating leaders do not believe that you build people up by tearing them down. Uplifting people are human stimulants who believe that taller structures are built by construction instead of destruction. Like effective parents, they raise their teams instead of lowering them.

The reason why true motivating leaders spend so much energy on people development is because they see that the success of a team is related to the strengths and resources of its people. When people are encouraged to grow and to contribute, they function at higher levels, and they use more of their resources in creation and less in defense. The motivating leader is a people builder who is always on the "construction" site. Unfortunately, most people seem to feel that they have had leaders and managers who tried to motivate out of threats, criticism, nitpicking, and finding flaws or mistakes. Why do so many leaders lose their positive potential to influence by taking the people destruction course?

77

Mistaken Leadership Beliefs on How to Motivate

Think of past leaders or managers who were in tune to mistakes and removed from the things you did correctly. Why did they somehow or another miss the obvious—that motivation through intimidation, fear, or negativism is at best temporarily successful. Negative leadership is destructive and leads to poor morale, direct rebellion, or passive aggressiveness. There are a number of reasons why these individuals were unaware of better ways, and it will serve us well to take a brief look at the mistaken beliefs of negative leaders.

Mistaken Leadership Belief #1

If anything goes wrong, I, as the leader, will be blamed. Therefore, I must look over my people's shoulders and watch them every step of the way to quickly point out their mistakes (*threatened*).

Mistaken Leadership Belief #2

It is my job as leader to know more than anyone else. Since I am supposed to be the expert here, I can show my expertise best by criticizing, correcting, and spotting weakness (*know-it-all*).

Mistaken Leadership Belief #3

Spotting disabilities, inefficiencies, and flaws was the way I was raised, and look at me today. Besides, if you build up people's egos, they'll get swelled heads and become unmanageable (*dominator*).

Mistaken Leadership Belief #4

I assume a perfect performance. Why should I recognize someone who did what was expected of them? Besides, a paycheck is all they need to be motivated (*perfectionist*).

The Threatened Leader

When a leader is under a perceived threat (whether or not the threat is real does not matter), the stress experienced causes the person to react to errors in an exaggerated way. Any mistake is magnified. Instead of dealing with an error in a rational way (let's correct it or at least make the best of where we are right now), threatened leaders deal with mistakes irrationally (name-calling, withdrawal, sulking, revenge).

Tension builds on a team led by a threatened leader, although there is no research in support of this statement. It would be interesting to determine if there is greater turnover of personnel and more emotional problems among the ranks of threatened leaders. Certainly threatened leaders of organizations where people volunteer and can quit at will lose their power because they lose their membership. This result has been observed in everyday life by many people.

What the threatened leader fails to realize is that the power to solve organizational problems exists within the team. People under threat live defensively. Defensive people defend rather than create. The creation of new ideas is the answer to mistakes. Threatened leaders thus find themselves in a Catch-22 situation. They receive no new ideas from members who are threatened; no new ideas means no progress. In their study of America's top corporations, Tom Peters and Robert Waterman point out that good companies allow and even encourage mistakes, hoping that decisions are right more than 50 percent of the time. Threatened leaders want right decisions 100 percent of the time, and so they make very few decisions. Threatened leaders truly do make fewer mistakes!

The Know-It-All Leader

The know-it-all leader is also threatened and tries to cover up his or her feelings of inadequacy by believing the impossible notion that "I must know more than anyone else here since I am the boss. If anyone challenges an idea of mine, it is a personal attack on me. If anyone asks me a question that I can't answer, my leadership is challenged. I can avoid being challenged by attacking first and spotting the other person's weaknesses. If I can spot something wrong that someone else did, I will establish my superiority." This type of leader is guided by the erroneous notion that "the more I show them how wrong they are, the more they will respect me."

A newly appointed elementary school principal feels threatened by being caught in the know-it-all syndrome and seeks help. "You see, doctor, I taught fifth grade for years. While I was good at it, now, as principal, I don't know anything about kindergarten or first, second, third, fourth, or sixth grade. I live in constant fear that one of my teachers may come into my office and ask me a question about one of those grades and what they should be doing. What if I don't know the answer? I just know that the teacher would go running to the faculty room and tell everyone that I, the principal, didn't know the answer."

"I think you have it wrong, Jim," replies the doctor. "Your job as principal is not to know more than the kindergarten teachers. If there is an expert in kindergarten in your school, that expert better be in the kindergarten classroom! Your job as leader is to help the teachers become experts in what they do by building them, encouraging them to develop better ideas, and motivating them. A leader is an expert—an expert in motivating people. You are putting too much of a burden on yourself and making what could be an exciting and challenging job a painful experience."

The Dominating Leader

Some leaders believe that it is their role to spend most of their energies correcting. This is due to cultural reasons in that this is the way that much of society functions, and most of the models in the lives of dominating leaders were probably correctors. Parents tell a young child who puts her shoes on by herself for the first time, "They're on the wrong feet," rather than "Wow, you put your own shoes on all by yourself. What an achievement for a three-year-old! Can you show us how you did that? You must be proud of yourself."

School teachers tend to mark the number of wrong answers instead of the number of correct answers. Police officers give tickets for speeding as opposed to commendations for staying within the legal limit. Signs in public parks read "no fires, no alcohol, no littering" rather than "enjoy yourself and experience the beauty of nature." Weather forecasters tell us that there is a 20 percent chance of rain instead of an 80 percent chance of sunshine. People often give directions by saying, for example, "turn at the fourth red light." Why do they pessimistically conclude that all of those lights will be red? There's a 50 percent chance that they'll be green! These are all examples of a cultural bias toward negative focusing.

The dominating leader has not taken time to break out of the cultural mold and responds like everyone else does. If you take just a few minutes to think of it, there are alternative ways of leading people and of building them to strengthen the total team. Some alternative ways of building people will be discussed shortly, but first consider the fourth mistaken belief of discouraging leaders, perfectionism.

The Perfectionist Leader

The perfectionist leader assumes that everyone will do a perfect job and that no one needs to be recognized for his or her efforts or achievements. "Only weaklings need a pat on the back," "If you compliment someone, you are likely to spoil them," and "A paycheck is the only reward a person needs" are some of the naive conclusions drawn by discouraging leaders. In *Turning People On,* I suggest that the positive information that a leader has about a person's achievements is meaningless unless it is communicated to that person (L. Losoncy, 1977).

Silence is not golden when we want to encourage people. The encouraging leader does not assume that people know they are doing well. Failure to communicate positives may lead to discouragement. Many people go through an entire day without receiving any encouragement. The person who cooks meals, does his or her homework, takes out the garbage, an so on is frequently not acknowledged, but just assumed.

In organizations, people start to withdraw their services when unmotivated. Confrontation may then be the only intervention that appears appropriate. The situation could have been avoided by a more positive style that did not assume perfection but rather showed appreciation for it.

Motivating leaders avoid leadership problems by building people. Eight approaches to being an uplifting leader who builds people are discussed in this chapter:

- Re-imaging
- Image analyzing
- Asset focusing
- Converting
- Special-izing
- Best foot forwarding
- Un-assuming
- Underwhelming

These approaches may be appropriate for dealing with the following problems:

1. Poor morale
2. Lack of confidence

3. Burnout
4. Perfectionism
5. Negative self-image
6. Feeling insignificant or unimportant
7. Lack of motivation
8. Irresponsibility
9. Change

Approach #7: Re-imaging

Re-imaging involves building teammates by encouraging the development of a more positive self-image. Re-imaging is self-image modification.

The major cost of the "building up by tearing down" leadership approach is the self-image of the membership. Self-image has been demonstrated to be the major determinant of achievement and performance.

The leader who believes in building people starts by building the self-image of, or re-images, the unmotivated. Re-imaging grew out of the work of Maxwell Maltz, the plastic surgeon who wrote *Psycho-Cybernetics*. Maltz concluded:

> When self-image changes, everything in life changes. Researchers have shown that students have gone from "F" grades to "A's" in a matter of weeks. Salespeople have literally doubled their income, shy people have become respected leaders, depressed people have developed a renewed enthusiasm for life (Maltz, 1960).

All of these changes took place because of changes in self-image or re-imaging. One study after another has demonstrated the power of one's self-image on performance. Self-image appears of be even more important than I.Q. in determining achievement. Some studies indicate that changes in a person's self-image lead to changes in achievement. Again, this is powerful news. A motivating leader, a builder of people, realizes that performance is preceded by the belief that "I can." K.L. Harding (1966) showed that it could be predicted with reasonable certainty whether or not a student would quit school just by knowing the student's self-image.

A better gauge than any test devised to determine how a person will perform in a position is the person's self-image. Relating these astounding findings to achievement in school, William Purkey, the father of self-image research, writes:

> The conclusion seems unavoidable—a student carries with him certain attitudes about himself and his abilities, which play the primary role in how he or she performs in school (Purkey, 1970).

Have you ever observed a person labeled stupid or slow by one person (the leader) in the presence of another person who believed in him or her? This same person performs like two different people in the two different settings. He or she performs at a higher level in the presence of the believer. The believer is a self-image builder. Maltz writes:

> The self-image is the key to the personality and to human behavior. Change the self-image and you change the personality and behavior. But more than this, the self-image sets the boundaries of individual accomplishment. It defines what you can and cannot be. Expand the self-image, and you expand the area of the possible. The development of an adequately realistic self-image will seem to imbue the individual with new capabilities, new ideas, and literally turn failure into success (Maltz, 1960).

Maltz's classic findings are as relevant today as they were when he wrote them. Keep in mind the power of self-image on achievement that these research studies indicate. A negative-oriented leader literally alters self-image in negative directions, which causes anxiety, apprehension, and feelings of incompetence, all of which are inconsistent with long-term performance. The outcome can be otherwise, however, through a re-image approach of leadership.

Self-Image: A Person's Self-Definition

Think of self-image as follows. Imagine that a *Webster's Dictionary* representative approaches you and says, "I'd like to put you in our dictionary next year. Like all words in our dictionary, which have a definition behind them, we will need you to define yourself, so that the world can know you. For example,

> *Pencil:* a rod-shaped object filled with graphite or lead, used to write with.

> [*Your name*]: an intelligent person who at times lacks confidence, also panics when making a mistake; tends to be shy with people.

The self-definition is the self-image. It may be quite inaccurate and limiting, but a person nevertheless believes that it is written in granite and then proceeds through life treating the self-image as a fact. The self-image tends to evolve from past experience:

> *Second grade teacher*: "You are a bright child."

> *Sales manager*: "Your biggest problem is that you lack confidence and will never get anywhere without confidence." (The manager's theory is "I can scare you into gaining confidence," or the building up by tearing down syndrome.)

> *Parents*: "Unless you do something perfectly, don't do it at all" (panic when making mistakes).

> *Spouse*: "You are so shy with people, Why don't you come out of your shell?"

Your self-definition today is a result of your interpretation of your social experiences. Remember an encourager's five insights and the importance of people on people? The good news is that the leader is in an excellent position to build new, more constructive self-definition into an individual personality. This is called re-imaging.

The rest of the approaches in this chapter are various ways for a leader to re-image, or to build new self-definition to produce improved performance and, more importantly, a happier, more confident individual.

Approach #8: Image Analyzing

Image analyzing is analyzing the current self-image of the team or the teammates to uncover perceived strengths and limitations as a starting point for creating a new image.

To re-image, the leader needs to be aware of the team member's current self-image. This is achieved through an image analysis. Image analysis is an attempt to construct an individual's dictionary definition of who he or she is, including the positive and negative characteristics. An image analysis can be done in one of two ways:

1. The leader can infer by observation of behavior some of the components of a person's self-image.

2. The leader can actually ask members to write their own dictionary definitions of themselves.

Image Analysis by Observation

The leader of a small business that sells beauty products notices that Carol, a 45-year-old-woman who was originally turned onto selling, has produced no sales for a month. The leader thinks back and remembers a few of Carol's latest statements to analyze her image.

"Well, I'm going through this divorce now and I have to admit that I often wonder if I'm still attractive, and whether I will ever be loved again."

On another occasion, Carol said, "I took a chance and called this old college buddy up and invited him over for dinner, and he turned me down. I never called again."

With these two thoughts in mind, the sensitive leader realizes that Carol needs to be built up. Through image analysis, the leader determines Carol's self-definition to be:

> *Carol*: unappealing (yet selling beauty products), rejected, gives up after being turned down, lacks determination.

The image analysis helps the leader realize that Carol needs to be built up through re-imaging (see the upcoming approaches in the pages ahead). Re-imaging is a much better approach than pressuring, lecturing, or pointing out weaknesses.

Image Analysis Through Membership Participation

The leader can encourage members to do an image analysis at a staff meeting. The leader requests:

> I'd like you to imagine that a representative from *Webster's Dictionary* comes to you and says, "We at *Webster's* would like to put your name in the dictionary next year, but, like all of our words, we need a definition behind your name so that the world will know who you are. What definition would you put in back of your name to describe you? Think of traits and characteristics, such as outgoing, shy, and so on.

The leader then encourages the teammate to think of when and at what age these definitions became part of their individual self-image. By pointing out that the person wasn't born this way but became this way, the leader demonstrates that it is possible to develop new traits and characteristics.

The leader then asks the members to add some new definitions to their self-images and eliminate those that are counterproductive. The leader asks them how their new lives would look if they were this new way. The membership is encouraged to think of opportunities to act, based on the new self-image, to make these changes happen. People are then encouraged to report at the next meeting the progress they have made as a result of re-imaging.

Approach #9: Asset Focusing

Asset focusing is the process of focusing on a teammate's assets, strengths, and resources to build the person's self-image.

Some leaders are hindered by their inclination to see liabilities and mistakes. They see, as the adage goes, the glass of water as half empty rather than half full. These leaders tend to choose, select, or focus on the negatives. Negative focusing builds negative self-image. Negative self-image produces behavior consistent with that self-image.

"But," the owner and manager of a real estate agency says, "I have this one agent who has nothing, *nothing* good about him. What do I do to motivate him?" Think of that person who has nothing good about him or her. Slowly go over the following list and see if any assets come close to being appropriate. Then record them below. Start to lift up and bring in this down-and-out person by being an asset focuser.

_____

_____

_____

above-board
absorbing
abstract thinking
academic, scholarly
accepting
accessible
accommodating
accountable
achieving
action-oriented
adaptable, flexible
advanced, ahead-of-
  time
adventurous
affable
affectionate
alive
alongside
ambitious
amenable
amusing
approachable
artful
artistic
assertive
assiduous, hard-
  working
astute
at ease
attentive
authentic
authoritative
aware
balmy, smoothing
benevolent
benign
big-hearted
blissful
broad-minded
busy
calm

candid
capable
carefree
casual
cautious
character
charitable
charming
chic, fashionable
civil, polite
clarifier
clean
clear
clever
commanding
competent
comprehensive
concise
concrete thinker
confident
congenial
conscientious
contemporary
content
cooperative
cordial
courageous
courtly
creative
credible
critical
cultured
curious
daring
dazzling
decent
decisive
deep-thinking
deliberate
demanding
demonstrative

dependable
determined
devout
didactic
diligent
direct
domestic
dramatic
dreamer
dynamic
earnest
easy-going
economical
educated
effective
effervescent
eloquent
enduring
energetic
enlightening
enterprising
enthusiastic
ethical
even
exacting
exhaustive
expedient
explicit
expressive
fair
faithful
fearless
fervent
forceful
forgiving
forward
frank
frugal
fun-loving
futuristic
gallant

generous
genteel
genuine
gets along
giving
good-hearted
good-natured
graceful
gracious
grateful
gregarious
growing
guardian
guiding
guileless
gutsy
happy
hard-working
hardy
harmless
harmonious
healthy
heartening
helper
heroic
honest
honorable
hope-giving
hospitable
humanitarian
humorous
hygienic
idealistic
imaginative
impartial
improving
improvising
indefatigable
independent
indispensable
individualistic
industrious

informed
ingenious
innocent
inspiring
instructive
integrity
intellectual
intense
interesting
introspective
invaluable
inventive
invigorating
involved
judicious
kind
knowledgeable
laborious
lawful
leader
learned
lenient
level
liberal
likable
lively
loyal
magnanimous
matter-of-fact
meaning-giving
mediating
merciful
methodical
mild
mindful
mobile
moderate
modern
modest
moral
motivated
motivator

neat
negotiable
neighborly
neutral, impartial
noble
nourishing
objective
observant
open
organized
original
outstanding
participator
peaceful
perceptive
persevering
persistent
persuasive
philosophical
plausible
playful
pleasant
poised
polished
popular
positive
potent
powerful
practical
praiseworthy
precise
prepared
productive
proficient
profound
progressive
promising
prompt
proper
prosperous
protector
provider

punctual	sedate	task-oriented
purposeful	self-confident	teamworker
questioning	self-controlled	technical
quick-witted	sensitive	tenderhearted
quizzical	sincere	thorough
radiant	smooth	thoughtful
rapt	social	timeless
rational	soothing	tolerant
realistic	sophisticated	trained
reasonable	sparkling	tranquil
reassuring	specific	trendsetter
refined	spirited	trustworthy
reflective	spontaneous	truthful
rejuvenating	sporty	up-to-date
reliable	spunky	venturesome
religious	stable	veteran
remarkable	stalwart	vibrant
remindful	stately	visionary
reserved	staunch	vocal
resolute	stimulating	watchful
respectable	straightforward	well-adjusted
respectful	strong	well-read
responsible	studious	wholehearted
responsive	sturdy	willful
sagacious	stylish	wise
scholastic	succinct	witty
scrupulous	systematic	
seasoned	tactful	

Asset focusing involves being tuned into observing what is right with or what is a potential resource of another person. Asset focusing is an approach to help re-image an individual to have a more positive self-image. Asset focusing is a leader's way of building by constructing.

How could you as a leader make use of asset focusing on your team?

_____

_____

_____

Approach #10: Converting

Converting involves creatively "converting" a person's perceived liabilities, weaknesses, or at first glance negative characteristics into potential assets.

What if, after going over the preceding list, a leader concludes, "I still haven't identified any positive traits in this person to start to build him or her. In fact, this person only has negative qualities." Is hope lost? No, not for the creative motivating leader who wants to build. Converting is the next step. Converting is the process of changing negative traits by seeing the positive, applicable components of those traits and sharing the observation.

Look over the following negative traits and ask yourself if there is a positive silver lining in any of them:

1. Stubborn _____

2. Lazy _____

3. Foolishly daring _____

4. Troublemaker _____

5. Nosy _____

6. Gabby _____

7. Impulsive _____

8. Nit-picker _____

Is stubbornness a negative trait? Yes, in a way, but many people would want their heart surgeon to possess this same negative trait while operating on them. Is foolishly daring a negative trait? Yes, but all of the world's great entrepreneurs and great scientists dared to tread on unsafe ground. Every person who has made the world a better place with a breakthrough idea was foolishly daring.

The motivating leader who wants to build people can see things in them that go right over the heads of others.

A prison counselor who was sensitive to the use of converting observed:

> Yes, it is my job to help these prisoners leave jail and go out and function in the world. It's a hard task because their self-images are so negative that they believe they have no skill to offer society. So I take their very crimes and convert them to assets that may have been previously misdirected.
>
> The safe-cracker, for example, has manual dexterity, determination, courage, goal-directedness, dreams, love of work, wishes for a better tomorrow, hope, in many cases strong knees, good ears, ability to plan ahead, and certainly patience. I help them to see that if they take these same traits and channel them in the right direction, very few companies wouldn't want them.

Convert the very liabilities of a discouraged teammate into assets that are socially constructive and build, build, build.

Reflect for a few moments and convert some of your people's liabilities into assets.

_____

_____

_____

Approach #11: Special-izing

Special-izing is spotting a positive, "special" talent or characteristic in a teammate, such as a "claim-to-fame."

Special-izing is the process of identifying one person's uniqueness and sharing it with that person. This uniqueness is captured by observing the person's claim-to-fame.

Each one of your people has a bit of pride about something that he or she does well. This magical motivated feeling of "I'm good at so and so" may have to do with some talent either on or off the job. It really doesn't matter whether the person's claim-to-fame is "I'm really an organized person at work," "I won the company golf tournament for the past two years" or even "I'm a great grandma." What does matter is that you communicate your awareness of his or her claim-to-fame.

What are claims-to-fame? Claims-to-fame are proud moments of achievement in people's lives or even current talents or skills that they have. Claims-to-fame are also the sources of personal feelings of competence and uniqueness.

Children readily share their claims-to-fame with others: "I can run faster than anybody on my whole block" or "I'm really good at spelling. I won the spelling bee!" Adults, however, are less likely to share their sources of pride or talent with others, either because they are not even aware of their talents or because they feel that others just don't care. Be a caring, sensitive leader by listening to and watching your people with extended antennae that are fine-tuned to their sources of pride.

Notice how the listening manager differs from the discouraging manager in response to the same comments of an employee:

> *Employee*: You know my report that was due on Friday? I'll have it finished by Monday, four days early, Mr. Manager.

> *Discouraging manager*: OK, well, let me give you another report to work on then.

> *Encouraging manager* (who is tuned into claims-to-fame): You finished the report already, Tom? Great! That will give me more time to review what I wrote yesterday. You have a real respect for deadlines. I know I can always count on you.

Take another look at Tom's comment and the way he expressed his achievement. Put on your claims-to-fame–sensitive ears and eyes. Can you see and hear pride in Tom's accomplishment? The discouraging manager ignored the extra effort, which left Tom with the feeling that going the additional mile wasn't worth it. If Tom stays with this manager, he may wind up on our list of burned-out, discouraged employees in a short period of time. The encouraging manager, who saw Tom's pride in beating the deadline, turned it into a claim-to-fame. You can bet that Tom will continue to meet or beat deadlines in the future because it is part of his claim-to-fame and he was recognized by an encouraging manager. As a result of an encouraging manager, Tom is happy, the manager is happy, and the company is happy. Make your employees, yourself, and your company happy by recognizing your teammates' claims-to-fame.

Where Can You Use Special-izing with a Member?

Sense sources of strength by identifying the hidden resources in you team members. Be a talent scout! Spot not only the assets that are obvious, but imagine what hidden resources and undiscovered potential might also exist in your people.

At times, you may feel that one of your people is suffering from an energy crisis. Solve the energy crisis almost instantly by identifying the potential resources in the discouraged person. What are resources? Resources are the hidden assets that are not immediately obvious.

Identify resources in some of your people.

_____

_____

_____

_____

Approach #12: Best Foot Forwarding

Best foot forwarding is centering on a teammate's past or present or visualizing future performance at his or her best rather than at his or her worst.

Best foot forwarding is an approach to building people that can be credited to the late psychologist B.F. Skinner. It is allowing people who are feeling at their worst to re-experience themselves at their best by reinforcing past successes.

Successful, encouraging leaders deal with people quite differently than leaders of the past. Remember the old-time baseball manager, for example? Traditionally, the baseball manager would spend most of his time explaining to the hitter who was in a batting slump what he was doing wrong. "You're stepping in the bucket. You're taking your eye off the ball. Don't drop your shoulder. Don't stand away from the plate. Are you afraid of the fastball?"

Transfer yourself into the slumping hitter's spikes for a few moments and listen to your fault-finding manager's observations. Imagine that you have to step up to the plate against the league's toughest and fastest pitcher immediately after hearing these five comments from your manager. Would being bombarded by your manager's negative comments make you more capable and confident as you step into the batter's box?

> Maybe what the manager says is true. Maybe I am afraid of the fastball, but what if the ball is coming directly at me? What should I do? If I duck, the manager will be convinced that I'm gun-shy and pull me out of the lineup. And if I don't duck, maybe I'll get beaned.

Not only does focusing on what a person does wrong add confusion, anxiety, and tension, but, most importantly, it decreases the batter's self-confidence as he steps up to the plate.

The self-image's self-talk goes like this: "I'm in a bad hitting slump. And I'll bet that I'll never break out of it with all of these things wrong with me."

Modern, encouraging baseball managers employ a more effective style to help troubled batters out of a slump. A positive manager has videocassette recordings of some of the hitter's finest moments. Prior to stepping up to the plate, the batter turns on the videocassettes and watches his big hit, his winning grand slam, or his perfectly place bunt that brought the crowd to its feet and caught his dazed opponent off guard. The hitter hears his name announced over the public address system and steps up to the plate, this time with confidence. By observing what he did when his hitting was hot, the hitter subconsciously learns how to lift his shoulder and stand near the plate and remembers to go after the fastball aggressively with the winning feeling. Be a modern, encouraging manager by pointing out the talents and assets of your people.

Start by seeing the one thing that someone does right rather than the nine things that he or she does wrong. Tell the person. Then sit back and watch the strength and confidence you brought out in him or her. Propel the person to try to improve number two, then number three, and so on. Give people the feeling that "I can do it because there are a lot of things that are right with me. Let me put my best foot forward."

With which teammates could you use best foot forwarding?

_____

_____

_____

Approach #13: Un-assuming

Un-assuming occurs when the leader recognizes and shows appreciation for the everyday, routine work of the team rather than "assuming" or taking their performance for granted.

Un-assuming relates to one of the five insights about people from Chapter 2: People are motivated by recognition. Un-assuming is the process of occasionally recognizing and not taking for granted the routine everyday actions of the membership.

Louise, Anna, and Tom will never forget their unassuming leader:

> Louise, you have especially great talents in working with difficult clients. Your sensitivity in handling people is a real asset to us all. It's almost as if we have a resident psychologist here.
>
> Anna, I never saw anybody who could find those lost policies like you can. I'd personally appreciate it if you would share some of the techniques you use with some of the other employees to help them.
>
> Tom, thanks for keeping all of the spirits of the other real estate agents up during this difficult market time. Whenever you come into the office, you give us drowning folks a periscope to rise above the water and see the land of hope.

The leaders of these three people could have held their comments in, but instead chose to share their observations with Louise, Anna, and Tom. The leaders were in touch with their positive influencing powers. Be a "pick 'em up" type of person to your people. Don't assume—notice!

How could you make use of un-assuming today?

_____

_____

_____

Approach #14: Underwhelming

Underwhelming occurs when the leader shares how he or she has grown from the ideas of the team. Underwhelming is the opposite of overwhelming.

Underwhelming is a people-building approach I learned from Gust Zogas, a Pennsylvania college president. He didn't plan underwhelming to be a technique; it was a very natural style for him.

Underwhelming involves working with people with the opposite approach of bowling them over with your knowledge. Instead, underwhelming is turning to the team for their ideas. The underwhelming leader believes that the people on the team have the capacity to answer the demands of a situation.

Underwhelming is an approach that is limited to secure leaders. The underwhelming leader is strong enough to show weakness, secure enough to be real, and intelligent enough to know what he or she does not know.

Underwhelming builds people because the leader shows respect for the team's ability to play a part in finding a solution.

List some instances in which you can employ underwhelming.

_____

_____

_____

Ten Crucial Things To Remember and Ten Practical Things to Do from Chapter 4

MOTTO: Motivating leaders are people builders

1. **Remember:** People answer "yes" to the question, "In your past, were you more motivated by leaders who

saw your assets than those who say your liabilities?" so...
Do: Put your eye on the positive to build. Empower!

2. **Remember:** Don't put extra undue pressure on yourself by believing "I must know more than every person here," so...
    Do: Be prepared to learn from your team's ideas whenever possible. If you are asked a question to which you don't know the answer, simply respond, "I don't know. I will find out." What a non-defensive way of gaining respect! Empower!

3. **Remember:** The unmotivated person has a self-image problem which needs to be altered, so...
    Do: Begin a re-imaging program with your unmotivated or discouraged people to build them. Empower!

4. **Remember:** To re-image, observe a person's current self-image, so...
    Do: Construct a self-image analysis or have the person construct his or her own self-image or dictionary definition. Together, add positives and remove negatives and make a self-improvement plan for the person. Empower!

5. **Remember:** A person's behavior is a function of his or her self-image. Negative behavior is a product of a negative self-image, so...
    Do: Do an asset analysis by observing all of the assets in this chapter that could be relevant to a particular individual and share them. Empower!

6. **Remember:** Even liabilities in people can be converted into assets to build them, so...
    Do: Take a person's weakness and convert it into an asset by creative leadership. Show how that asset can tie into contributing to the goals of the organization. Empower!

7. **Remember:** In this age of depersonalization, where everyone is a number instead of a person, people have a need for uniqueness, so...
    Do: Special-ize people by identifying their unique claims-to-fame or proud moments in their lives. Empower!

8. **Remember:** A person who is down and out (slumping) will remain on the downward spiral unless someone turns him or her around, so...
    Do: Recall with the person some of his or her finer moments and identify some of the assets these moments demonstrated. Help that person put his or her best foot forward. Empower!

9. **Remember:** People have a strong need for recognition that is often lost in the routine, so...
    Do: Don't take performance for granted. Be an unassuming leader who recognizes and notices the efforts of others. Empower!

10. **Remember:** Overwhelming people with your knowledge intimidates the membership, so...
    Do: Turn people on by underwhelming them, and allow them to help find the solution. What a way to empower your team! Empower!

Motivating leaders build people. They empower!

5

PLANT POSITIVE PURPOSE IN PEOPLE

A day that will stand out in the history books for centuries to come is July 20, 1969. Do you recall what happened? It was the day when humankind's grasp became closer to its reach. It was the day when the citizens of the planet Earth placed their first person on the moon one quarter of a million miles away. It was a proud day for all earthlings.

July 20, 1969 was an especially proud day for me. Why should it have been more important for me than most other days? It was all because of a special meaning-giving leader for whom I worked. Let me explain the power of a meaning-giving leader.

In the summer months of 1963 to 1967, I was employed by Carpenter Technology, a Reading Pennsylvania-based steel company. My job responsibility was to bundle bars of steel over and over again for eight hours a day, five to six days a week. Sound boring? It could have been, but I was fortunate enough to have a farsighted foreman who helped point out to each of us bundles what we were really doing.

"Part of what you guys will be bundling today is headed for Detroit and will be used for making automobiles," the burly enthusiast would say at the beginning of the day. On another occasion, the seven-to-three crew was told that the steel bars we were bundling today were destined for a pharmaceutical company where they would be made into surgical equipment.

But the one meaning-giving day I remember the most was when Mr. U. confided, "This week most of what you fellas will be wrapping up to ship out is a specialty steel designed to be part of the spacecraft like the one that our government will eventually be landing on the moon!"

Well, I hope it doesn't sound corny to say, but on that July day when Neil Armstrong took his first step on the lunar surface, I was in the front row of the world's cheering section, looking back with pride on my exciting moments of bundling steel bars from seven to three o'clock, five days a week. I often wonder how many tens of thousands of people like myself contributed to the moon landing in some way, shape, or form—from secretaries, to mail persons, to janitors. Most of them probably never experienced the pride I did. Why? Because most contributors didn't have a manager like Mr. U., who took the time to share with his employees how their jobs affect the people of the community—or humanity! The leader planted positive purpose in our work.

People Need Purpose and Meaning

The deepest role of the leader is planting a bottomless purpose in the team's mission. The more vision the leader projects, the greater the team's motivation to dig in and give it their all. Some people just go to work; others on the same job experience their team making a contribution to the world. In "Creating Esprit de Corps," Jim Channon writes:

> Belonging to a group, especially to a group that is making a difference in the world, can be a powerful motivating factor. People who know they are working for something larger, with a more noble purpose, can

be expected to be loyal, dependable, and at a minimum, more inspired (Channon, 1992).

The leader who envisions his or her role as constantly articulating a vision that is aligned to the team's purpose rallies commitment to the team. This leader offers the members more than just a job; he or she adds meaning in their lives.

Leadership Means Giving Meaning and Purpose to People

In Search of Excellence, a book that every leader might want to come close to memorizing, goes to the bottom-line question: What type of leadership works and what type doesn't work?

Poorer performing companies focus on the numbers rather than on the product and the people who make and sell it. Top companies, on the other hand, always seem to recognize what the companies that only set financial targets don't know or don't deem important. The excellent companies seek to understand that every person seeks meaning (not just the top fifty who are in the bonus pool).

Peters and Waterman, the authors of *In Search of Excellence,* continue:

> Nietzche believed that "he who has a why to live for can bear almost any how." John Gardner observes in *Morale,* "Man is a stubborn seeker of meaning" (Peters and Waterman, 1984).

In *New Pathways in Psychology,* Colin Wilson writes:

> Man evolves through a sense of external meaning. When his sense of meaning is strong he maintains a high level of will-drive and of general health. Without this sense of external meaning, he becomes a victim of subjective emotions, a kind of dream that tends to degenerate into nightmares (Wilson, 1972).

Indeed, if we don't have a purpose "raising" us, we are orphans to life.

Planting Positive Purpose in People

Five meaning-gaining approaches to "raise" people are presented in this chapter:

- Home-ing in
- Meta-job describing
- Winding up
- Before and aftering people
- Un-menializing

These approaches are suggested as a way for you, the motivating leader, to help your teammates answer the question, "Why do I toil?" This chapter is especially relevant for the following problems:

1. Burnout
2. Apathy
3. Closed-mindedness
4. Drug/alcohol problems
5. Organization stagnation
6. Loss of meaning
7. Questioning, "Why do I do this?"
8. Lack of motivation

Approach #15: Home-ing In

Home-ing in is sensitively understanding a teammate's outside-of-work context at home as a factor in the person's attitude and performance.

Home-ing in is a leadership tool designed to more effectively understand people by understanding their pressures, frustrations, achievements, interests, hobbies, and values outside of work. I learned about home-ing in as a counselor. I wondered why some students performed nowhere near their potential and decided to visit them in their homes. In the settings where they lived, I listened to them reflect about the school. The insight shook me like a southern California earthquake. Their lives outside of school were much closer to home in their life priorities. I never would have had that insight without home-ing in. I understood their situation and their lack of motivation more clearly. Lack of motivation is lack of meaning.

Think for a moment about some of your people. When they meet someone for the first time at a social gathering and are asked what they do for a living or what organization they are involved in, do they put their fingers in front of their mouths and apologetically mumble a few words, quickly hoping that the conversation will move on to a more interesting topic? Or, do their shoulders open up like a peacock displaying its feathered finery as they proudly speak of their contribution to the company, the team, and society?

Through home-ing in, a leader can get an inside scoop from the outside. This gives the leader a better perspective in understanding the feelings and meaning of a person, to learn if he or she finds fulfillment on the team.

Use home-ing in with your most discouraged people. How would they describe their contribution to your organization to a friend?

_____

_____

_____

Approach #16: Meta-job Describing

Meta-job describing involves giving people greater purpose and meaning by reframing their contribution to their own professional development, to their team, to the organization, and to the world.

The highly respected Springfield, Illinois barber-stylist was asked for the formula to his secret for success in giving haircuts. "Oh, I don't give haircuts," he responded, "I give courage and confidence and hope." He loved his work and he knew his contribution. That's why he was successful! He knew that the haircut was the physical thing that he did, and he knew that a good haircut led to some results that went beyond the physical into the metaphysical.

The sensitive police chief turned to his men and women after a tough holiday season, when the demands placed on them are heavy, and shared this thoughts: "Most people in the community drove the roads and went to bed feeling safe this holiday season because of your efforts. A lot of people see you negatively, thinking that your job is to hassle and give tickets. But what you really give to most people is a deeper feeling of security, justice, and caring. If they are wronged, they call on you and you'll respond. The holiday season was better because of you. Thanks."

Does a hairdresser give a haircut—or confidence? Does a law enforcement officer give tickets—or security? Does a teacher give discipline—or knowledge? Does the Statue of Liberty give a pretty picture—or a theme of freedom? Does a doctor give a checkup and a prescription—or a feeling of potential wellness? Do the Scouts give medals— or a feeling of competence? Does an artist give a painting—or inspiration? Does a coach give a strategy—or a winning attitude? Does a husband or wife bring a paycheck home—or love? Does a company give just a paycheck—or meaning with the paycheck? The difference between the physical and the meta-physical is above and beyond. Give your people a raise by showing how their efforts affect themselves, the organization, and people in general.

While employed as a consultant to a publishing company that had low morale in the stock and order-filling departments, something struck me as quite interesting. In exploring their jobs with the resistant employees, I discovered that these people didn't really know what a contribution they were making through their jobs.

In meeting with the workers, I decided to "life-up" their jobs by helping them to see some of the "fringe benefits" of what they do. "Every day of your lives here at work is significant. Each and every day when you folks take books out of stock and send them out to successfully complete an order, some human being becomes satisfied. And each day there are people who await the arrival of their ordered packages of books. They need you! And each book that you send out has the capability of changing lives, from depression into joy, from boredom into meaning."

I congratulated the people who are world changers and told them that each day they change the quality of people's lives. I concluded by adding that people in their capacity have changed the quality of my life, because I am an author, and authors need them more than anyone! No stock people means no sales.

Because the stock and order-filling people were never told what a significant contribution their jobs made, their work and their feelings of satisfaction were reduced to simply putting books into boxes. Give your employees a raise by showing them how their efforts affect themselves, their organization, and humanity in general.

Meta-job describing means seeing people's contributions at a higher lever to instill purpose and meaning. For example:

Responsibility	Physical	Meta-physical
switchboard operator	answer phones	first voice of the company
vitamin sales consultant	sell vitamins	————————
secretary	type, file	————————
teacher	give facts	————————
clergy	give sermons	————————

How can you make use of meta-job describing in your leadership capacity?

———————————————————————————

———————————————————————————

———————————————————————————

Approach #17: Winding Up

Winding up occurs when the leader gets the team enthused about the day's potential achievements.

When a clock stops ticking, people think nothing about winding it up again. Burned-out people have stopped ticking and need to be wound up. Winding up grew out of my curiosity as to why people can't wait to see the next day's episode of a soap opera. Imagine if a leader could find the motivation behind people who cancel doctor appointments, tell noisy relatives to leave the house, and miss college classes to watch the soaps. That leader could create quite a motivated membership by understanding the principles that soap operas use.

One of the techniques that the soaps use is to get you excited about what will happen the next day. They wind you up. "Do you think Erik will say yes tomorrow?" "John's wedding will be on tomorrow—I won't miss that to see if his ex-wife shows up." Then, tomorrow they do the same thing to the viewer, and God bless those who on

Friday have to wait three days instead of one to find out what happens.

Soap opera writers are motivators. They give you a reason, a purpose, and a motive to tune in at any cost. They get you involved and build anticipation. Winding up is the process of getting people to look forward to a day or a particular event or giving people a reason, purpose, or motive to be present and to be involved. The leader shows them that there is something in it for them.

Effective leaders and great teachers—teachers who take the time to tell their students about the special class the next day—use winding up. Parents can also use winding up. Imagine parents getting their little six-year-old wound up to go to school on a typical day by telling him something like this:

> Jimmy, your dad and I are so excited for you because today is another opportunity for you to get smarter. Today you will learn new spelling words for half an hour. You will be able to spell more words by this afternoon than you ever could before in your whole life. On top of that, you will learn about numbers for forty-five minutes. When you come home, your dad and I would love to see our son count higher than ever before. To top it off, you'll learn new things about the world of science. Remember that day when you showed us how airplanes fly? Aren't you going to learn about the planets today? Maybe the teacher will talk about Star Wars! Yes, Jimmy, your dad and I are so proud of you. It's just too bad that the first graders who are sick today won't learn all of those things. Well, son, we'll be waiting with some cookies and milk when you come home. Then we'll sit down and listen to what you've learned today. Let us take one last look at you, because we will never see you the same again. You'll be smarter!

Winding up is the style of inspiring leadership to help people find a reason, a purpose, or a motive to become involved. Winding up helps people see that "there's something in this for me" (other than just a paycheck or fulfilling an obligation).

How could you use winding up with your people today?

_____

_____

_____

Approach #18: Before and Aftering People

Before and aftering people is the process of showing a teammate or the team where they were in the past (before) and how they have progressed to where they are now (after).

What do you know today that you didn't know yesterday? Last year at this time? Five years ago? When you were five? When you were born? You've come a long way, haven't you?

What will you know tomorrow that you don't know today? Next year at this time? Five years into the future? Ten years into the future? What will you know in your lifetime that you don't know now?

Before and aftering people is a concept that grew out of weight loss commercials, in which people point out how they looked before and how they look now. The effectiveness of the before–after leadership approach is that it builds pride in self-development and growth, pride that is often neglected. Before and aftering people is the process of showing an individual or the full membership where they were at some point in the past and where they have grown to be today.

Jill is a bit discouraged after a hard day. Her leader notices this and decides to before and after Jill the next day. The next morning her leader causally comments, "I was thinking about you yesterday, Jill, and how far you've come since you've been here. You've gone from trainee to crew chief, to swing manager, to assistant manager, and now manager! That's incredible progress. At this rate, where will you be in a year to two?"

The vice-president of administration tells his general manager and managers, "Our department is the back-bone and supporting system of this company. My three-year goal is for us to receive the respect we deserve and not take a back seat to any other department." The vice-president in this case is using the *before* as today and the *after* as in the future. In this form, before and aftering people has the effect of motivating to achieve future goals. They now have a purpose.

How can you use before and aftering in your organization?

Approach #19: Un-menializing

Un-menializing is the leader's constant reminder to the team members about the importance of their work and how it fits into the growth of the organization.

One heart surgeon conducted ten bypass operations a week for five years, a total of over 2000 operations. The complicated task had become routine, however, and, believe it or not, the surgeon was starting to become bored. All jobs if done over and over again can lead a person to put himself or herself on automatic pilot.

Leaders un-menialize when they occasionally remind the membership of the importance of their contribution to the organization, the overall society, and their own development. A general rule of thumb is the more routine a responsibility, the more the leader needs to un-menialize the task. This is especially important when quality appears to be slipping. In this case, the leader shows the membership the *positive implications* of good quality for the organization, the community, and themselves.

Think of all of the different titles of the people who look to you for leadership. How could you un-menialize the burned-out?

Title	*Un-menializing plans*
_____	_____
_____	_____
_____	_____

Ten Crucial Things to Remember and Ten Practical Things to Do from Chapter 5

1. **Remember:** Society is changing drastically. While people were formerly motivated by material gains, today people want meaning and purpose in their lives, so...
   Do: Be the leader who plants positive purpose.

2. **Remember:** Alienation and burnout are the result of lack of personal meaning in what a person does, so...
   Do: Let a picture of each of your people flash through you mind, as though they were on a slide carousel. Mentally, be an outsider. Go to each person's home and ask, "How important is your work?" (home-ing). Imagine each person's response. This will be a starting clue to tell you in whose spirits meaninglessness is living. Jot down the names of those who need a "booster shot" from you.

3. **Remember:** Lift discouraged spirits by giving team-mates meaning and purpose in what they do. First

of all, you must have genuine meaning and purpose yourself, so...

Do: Make sure you believe in the importance of your own responsibilities. If you feel ho-hum about the significance of what you do, the contagion of the yawn will be witnessed throughout the people environment. Second, walk with the conviction that what we do is important. Third, talk up the importance and significance of specific projects. For example, "This year our company is turning its eyes to you people to find new ways of..." Fourth, when you lose meaning and purpose, have a built-in plan to fire up your spirits again, for example, further education, motivation classes, and so on.

4. **Remember:** The motivated person is one who feels "what I do is important," so...

   Do: Dig deeper into what each of your employees actually does (meta-job describing). Do this by thinking about the importance of what each person contributes.

5. **Remember:** There are many ways to look at any job. The drab leader inspires in black and white; the meaning-giving leader inspires in rich shades of color, so...

   Do: Describe a job in its fullness:

Drab manager sees job	*Meaning giving manager uses meta-job describing*
a switchboard operator	the first voice of the company
a secretary	the very vehicle of communication to the outside world
a teacher	a molder of the future
a salesperson	the key to the company's future

See a responsibility in its colorful fullness and communicate meaning to each specific teammate's role.
Jot down every level you now have, and write out the
specific job. Don't just give a simple black-and-white
description; put your meaning-giving ad in "color."

6. **Remember:** In the old days, when a car broke down,
an ineffective way to get it working again was to kick
it. The effective way to get it started was to grab the
crank and wind it up, so...
Do: Wind up your burned-out people. Enthuse them
about what they will learn and achieve. Give them
meaning, purpose, and a motive to be there.

7. **Remember:** One way of building trust and planting
positive meaning and purpose in people is to be a
credit-giving leader, so...
Do: Never miss an opportunity to give public and
private credit to the achievers, the idea-givers, and
every contributor, from the receptionist to the
janitor.

8. **Remember:** Sometimes people can't see themselves
progressing and find themselves in a rut, so...
Do: Before and after people by enthusiastically
pointing out their progress (in position, in skills, in
attitude) since they joined the organization.

9. **Remember:** People make the difference in achieving
the team's goals, so...
Do: Show your teammates how they have "made the
difference" by pointing out to them very specific
instances where their efforts brought about the
achievement of goals (un-menialize).

10. **Remember:** Your people often do not understand
why you have asked them to do something that
appears to be "just additional grief" or the "hard
way." The reason for this lack of understanding is
that they don't have your perspective. When this
lack of understanding occurs, people become dis-

couraged and feel that you are just giving them extra hassles, so...

Do: Un-menialize by giving your people purpose to go the extra mile by showing them, very specifically, why you have to take the long road this time. Help them to see that you, too, would like to take short-cuts, but sometimes the extra effort is necessary.

Plant positive purpose in people. Spark you people's positive attitudes by bringing meaning into your team. Then, keep the fires within your people stoked by communicating your belief in them and your positive expectations of their achievements.

6

CREATE A WINNING TEAM FEELING

The poet Goethe suggested, "If you want someone to develop a specific trait treat them as though they already had it." In *In Search of Excellence,* Peters and Waterman state, "Label a man a loser and he'll start acting like one." In their study of the characteristics and attitudes present in America's top corporations, these authors conclude:

> The message that comes through so poignantly...is that we (employees) like to think of ourselves as winners. The lesson that the excellent companies have to teach is that there is no reason why we can't design systems that continually reinforce this notion: most of their people are made to feel that they are winners (Peters and Waterman, 1984).

That winning mood is best determined by leadership's attitude and expectations. Low expectations communicate a disbelief in people. Respect, on the other hand, is a belief in people communicated by leadership. "I believe in you. You are made of the stuff that gets things done." Winning coaches always expect to win. They show it, they act it, they communicate it.

Losing leaders don't expect to win. They tolerate

minimal performance and ignore small successes in order to build bigger successes. They aren't present on the scene to inspire and to urge onward. Leaders who create the losing feeling are satisfied with the status quo. Isn't it amazing how we have come to accept mediocrity and less than 100 percent performance?

Phil Crosby, author of *Quality Is Free,* describes how in most instances we expect mistakes and aren't even disappointed when they happen. We buy a bicycle with a few parts missing...our meal is served cold...the new carpeting arrives in the wrong color...the salesman makes twelve instead of fifteen calls...the doctor arrives twenty minutes late...the switchboard operator cuts us off...the service station attendant doesn't wash the windshield...our order is misunderstood...the secretary in the reception area doesn't smile, and on and on.

Crosby goes on to say that quality of service and performance is not something out of the ordinary. It's not an extra, and it's not just a good idea. It is simply giving people what they expect, what they paid for, or what was agreed to in a contract—no more, no less.

A hamburger at McDonald's, Burger King, or Wendy's is quality because it is consistent, with little variation each time. It's what we expect. Leadership demanded that standard of quality and went about making it happen. That is why very few of these major chains close down. Leadership set a goal, expected the goal to be achieved, and empowered its people with belief. There are many similar examples of successful leadership.

Disney didn't want Disneyland or Disney World to become a dirty amusement park. Compare the cleanliness at either park to the cleanliness of any major city.

Leadership-communicated expectations is the major factor in determining the performance and the winning or losing attitude of the membership. The influence of one's expectation on others is demonstrated not just in the corporation, but in education, psychotherapy, and medicine as well.

Expectation and Teacher Leadership

Research studies have shown that teachers who have positive expectations for students actually produce greater student achievement. When bogus psychological reports were given to teachers, telling them that the I.Q. scores of individuals were higher than they really were, the teachers' elevated expectations of the students' abilities led to greater student achievement. In *The Unconscious Conspiracy: Why Leaders Can't Lead,* Warren Bennis (1978) states, "In a study of school teachers, it turned out that when they had high expectations of their students, that alone was enough to cause an increase of twenty-five points in the students' I.Q. scores."

Robert Schuller, founder of the concept of "possibility thinking," reported on an elderly school teacher from New York who had a high rate of success with students whose peers had a much higher frequency of brushes with the law. When asked for the secret of her success, the teacher said, "I just loved those kids and believed in them."

If someone believes in me and communicates that belief to me along with understanding and a feeling that what I do is important, I will have a tendency to take a second look at myself. Down deep I want that person to be right, so I may try to make it happen. The fact that some psychologists tell us that we use only two to fifteen percent of our potential demonstrates that there is always room for improvement—in the context of an encouraging leader or teacher.

Expectation and Psychotherapeutic Leadership

What a teacher expects is, more often than not, what he or she will get. But the power of expectation goes way beyond the classroom and extends into the counseling therapist's office. Psychiatrist Frieda Fromm-Reichman concluded that the major factor in determining whether a patient would or would not get better is the psychotherapist's expectations about the patient's prognosis. The leader in the therapist's office can literally communicate a winning or losing feeling with the patient almost unobtrusively. One therapist might say, "You're the kind of person who can pull yourself out of depression. You can get yourself out of the house, join a social organization, get out and meet people, and develop your writing skills that you gave up in this depression. I believe in you." A different therapist might say, "You're too fragile to go out on your own now." Imagine the different outcomes!

This power of people on people is totally consistent with the social comparison theory as advanced by Leon Festinger. Basically, social comparison theory argues that humans, in the absence of some objective standard by which they can evaluate themselves, will compare themselves to other fellow humans. It is from this comparison that they draw their conclusions about their worth. When the psychotherapist, a perceived objective standard, communicates a respect for the patient, that person is more likely to move toward fulfilling those expectations. A therapist can communicate a winning feeling. What the therapist expects is, more often than not, what he or she will get.

Expectation and Medical Leadership

In *Persuasion and Healing,* Jerome Frank (1961) discusses the power of the doctor's expectations on the patient's cure. Numerous studies describe the effects of the placebo (a sugar pill) combined with guarantees from the doctor that "this pill will eliminate your symptoms." By communicating positive expectations, the doctor can influence the outcome.

In *Anatomy of an Illness,* popular writer Norman Cousins describes how he was told he had a disease that had never been cured before. How's that for creating hopeless expectations and a losing feeling? Norman Cousins was fortunate enough to find a doctor with positive expectations and a sense of hope. These positive expectations became the sources of energy that propelled Cousins onward to search for the cure. He reasoned that if negative thinking and a negative environment could produce symptoms of disease, why couldn't the reverse be true? Could surrounding oneself with a positive environment lead to good health? He started his "laughing cure" by bringing in Allen Funt of "Candid Camera." Cousins also took massive dosages of vitamin C. He checked out of the hospital and was eventually totally cured of a disease that no one else had ever survived. He tried new approaches because he had a medical leader who gave him hope and the winning feeling. As John Dryden wrote, "When there is no hope there can be no endeavor." I'd like to add: When there is some hope there may be an endeavor. I always like "maybes" better than "nos."

Leaders create moods through their communicated expectations. Tolerance of less than the best is a clear message. Inspiring by striving for excellence, building pride, communicating respect, and showing confidence creates the winning feeling.

Creating a Winning Feeling by Expecting the Best

The fields of education, psychotherapy, and medicine have demonstrated the importance of creating a winning feeling by expecting the best. We could add to those fields athletics, parenting, friendship, and any other areas where two people meet and communicate expectations and ideas.

Great leaders have great expectations. A number of approaches to create a winning feeling by expecting the team's best are presented in this chapter:

- Respect-ability
- Delegating
- "Can" opening
- Expectation altering
- Changing spotlights

This chapter is particularly relevant for the following problems:

1. Low self-esteem
2. Loss of belief in a particular person
3. Irresponsibility
4. Poor work quality
5. Low morale
6. Excuses
7. Feelings of being overwhelmed by problems
8. The "low on the totem pole" feeling

Approach #20: Respect-ability

Respect-ability is communicating to a teammate or the team "I believe in you. You can do it."

Respect-ability is the overall ability of a leader to convey respect and confidence in the team members. A lowly respectable leader tends to have little respect and confidence in the membership's potential. A highly respectable leader has a great deal of respect and confidence in the membership. It might be noted that both the lowly and highly respectable leaders tend to be accurate.

One way of assessing whether a person is willing and able to respect the membership is through the Leader's Respect-ability Scale. Take a few minutes and assess your current feelings about the membership.

Leader's Respect-ability Scale

1. Do I sometimes take over other people's responsibilities because I basically believe that they would mess up the job if I left it to them?
   YES ☐   NO ☐

2. Do I enlist my people's involvement in making decisions on ways to achieve the team's goals?
   YES ☐   NO ☐

3. Do I delegate responsibilities confidently to my people and believe that they can do it?
   YES ☐   NO ☐

4. Do I constantly communicate to my superiors or believe myself that I need more competent people in order to achieve what is expected of me as the leader?
   YES ☐   NO ☐

5. Do I allow some freedom and independence in the way my team goes about tackling its tasks?
   YES ☐   NO ☐

6. Do I believe that the teammate who is frequently late has within himself or herself the ability to find a way to be on time?
   YES ☐   NO ☐

7. Do I believe that with some empowerment, the uncooperative, resistant teammate can become a cooperative, involved team member?
   YES ☐   NO ☐

8. Do I believe that my least productive team member has more ability than he or she has previously shown?
   YES ☐   NO ☐

9. Do I believe that my lowest producing person can produce more?
   YES ☐   NO ☐

10. Do I believe that I can correct and discipline my least productive team member in a way that he or she can accept it, understand it, and become a productive contributor?

YES ❏   NO ❏

Now, score your answers for the number of R (respect responses). For each question that is relevant for you, add one point to your score.

1. No   6. Yes
2. Yes   7. Yes
3. Yes   8. Yes
4. No   9. Yes
5. Yes   10. Yes

1–3   Low respect
4–6   Average respect
7–8   High respect
9–10   Strong respect for your employees

Analyze your ten responses and jot down a plan to improve your respect-ability.

Approach #21: Delegating

Delegating involves constantly analyzing teammates to sense who would be capable of taking on higher level responsibilities, training them, encouraging them, and then celebrating their achievements with them.

Delegating grew out of the writing of Robert Townsend. Townsend made a convincing case that decisions and responsibilities in any organization should be made at the lowest possible level. Sometimes decisions like how many pencils to order are made at too high a level and consume time that could be better used elsewhere. Townsend suggested studying your organization to find the lowest possible level at which decisions could effectively be made. If additional training is needed at that level, provide it. That's just smart economics.

In this book on motivation, delegating is advocated for an additional reason: *delegating implies respect for someone else's abilities.* Delegating does involve risk at first, but over the long run it helps people grow and become more of a part of the total operation. As one great delegator said, "I would like my people to know everything I know so that I can move on to new issues." That person was vice-president of a Pennsylvania college. When he delegated, he gave the person additional credit. His secretary signed letters sent out to applicants in her name, not his. She was an involved part of the Student Services Department.

One of the greatest delegators I ever met was Edna Nash, a Vancouver, B.C. psychologist who was past president of the North American Society for Adlerian Psychology. As local president years later, she had responsibility for enlisting help to conduct conventions. At the same time, she had a private practice in psychology and still managed to run one of the smoothest conventions. After congratulating some of the responsible participants, I asked them where they got their experience in facilitating conventions.

"Oh, I had never done anything like this before," one proud woman responded. "You see, I went to talk to Edna about some changes I was going through in my life because I was becoming increasingly apathetic. Edna told me we could talk about that later. First, she had a job for me—to help conduct this convention. I panicked, explaining I could never do it. She insisted, and here I am."

Edna Nash knew how being given responsibility can really benefit a person. Edna delegated. Delegating involves analyzing the people in your organization to see who would be capable of taking on higher level responsibilities, training them, encouraging them, and then celebrating their achievements with them.

List your personnel. Do an asset analysis on each (see Chapter 4). After looking at each person's assets, what additional responsibilities do you think he or she could take on if you delegated them?

_____

_____

_____

Approach #22: "Can" Opening

"Can" opening is a leadership approach designed to create a winning feeling in a teammate by showing the person that he or she has much more potential than they previously thought.

When the leader hears the words "I can't" (especially after delegating), it is a clue that the leader needs to help the person grow by overcoming the "can't." The leader becomes a "can" opener. "Can" opening is a leadership approach designed to create a winning feeling in a person by showing the person that he or she is much more capable than they previously thought. The leader points out that most *can'ts* are not accurate. People really mean "right now I can't" and not "I could never." All of us in our past had times when we thought, "I can't walk," "I can't drive," "I can't dance," "I can't speak in public," "I can't read," or "I can't write."

Most can'ts have some common elements:

1. Each statement is an echo of an individual's current self-image. For example, "I can't speak in public" is a personal belief based on a past conclusion and is an attempt to make conclusions of the past fit into the future.

2. Each self-image statement is inaccurate, that is, it can be disproved. As you look closely at some can'ts

("I can't walk," "I can't read," or even "I can't quit smoking"), you will see that each conclusion could be challenged.

3. Although each self-image statement is inaccurate, the speaker is not consciously aware that the comment is inaccurate and proceeds through life as if the pronouncement were carved in his or her behavioral granite. The opinion of self is treated by the person as if it were a fact.

4. Each self-image *can't* statement limits the individual's potential achievements. As long as the person believes this personal opinion to be a fact, no growth can occur for that exact period of time.

5. With the help of a leader who uses the "can" opening approach, the individual can see that:

   a. He or she drew a false conclusion about his or her potential based upon experiences of the past.

   b. Because this person couldn't do the task yesterday doesn't mean that he or she won't be able to do it tomorrow.

   c. When this person started in the organization, there were responsibilities that he or she thought they couldn't handle then but have since mastered.

   d. The person has a choice. He or she can continue to believe "I can't," which will lead to no attempt. The result is nothing—no growth. On the other hand, he or she can believe "I can" ("can" opening) and proceed to make it happen. Making mistakes is like taking a first step; they simply need to be correct. The result is growth.

The "can" opening leader actually enhances the self-image of individuals and propels them to greater achievements. The winning feeling is created every time a person sees himself or herself growing.

With which individual could you use "can" opening? How could you proceed?

_____

_____

_____

Approach #23: Expectation Altering

Expectation altering involves enhancing one's leadership expectations of a teammate or the team.

William Glasser, founder of Reality Therapy, had an interesting perspective on human behavior. Glasser's views that "people are responsible" and "one person's behavior influences another's action" have influenced the ideas of leadership with encouragement (see the five insights in Chapter 2).

Glasser would communicate his respect for people by being intolerant of irresponsible behaviors. While many psychiatrists would analyze the catatonic patients who stood quietly with their arms rigidly at their sides, Glasser would tell them that he expected them to be able to stand normally and talk with him. He would point out how out of place they currently looked and that they could control it. Instead of accepting their irresponsible behavior, he altered his expectations of them—and told them. He expected them to act responsibly.

Expectation altering is an approach to change people's unproductivity by altering, in the leader's own mind, what the leader expects and then communicating the altered expectation.

The leader, as Glasser does, treats the person as if he or she can improve. "I believe in you" is a feeling that flows from the leader to the discouraged person. In this new vision, the leader communicates that "You are quite a capable person. I will treat you in the light of my new positive expectation. You can do it."

Using Expectation Altering to Create a Winning Feeling

Use expectation altering with your discouraged people to bring out the best in them. One way of making this concept practical on your team is as follows.

First, identify a few people who are marginally discouraged, for example, lacking confidence, unproductive, irresponsible, late, impolite with customers, and so on. List the specific behavior or attitude that each employee is exhibiting.

Discouraged employee	*Behavior, attitude*
Jo-Ann (typist-secretary)	Irresponsible (not specific enough). More specifically, she rarely meets deadlines and spends too much time speaking with the other employees.

After identifying the very specific signs of discouragement present in the person, bring the ideas discussed in the previous chapters of this book into the encouraging arena.

1. Understand and live in Jo-Ann's world for a few minutes. Do an I to you transfer and think about some of Jo-Ann's pressures, frustrations, needs, and goals (Chapter 3).

2. List some of Jo-Ann's strengths, assets, and resources (Chapter 4).

3. It is now time for an expectation alteration. Literally see Jo-Ann in your mind's eye as having the characteristics within her potential to be a responsible person who meets deadlines.

4. Schedule a special talk with Jo-Ann to convey your new expectation of her. You are now prepared to make a dramatic change in a person's behavior in just a few minutes.

When Jo-Ann arrives, start by showing her how you understand her world. For example, you might say, "I guess there are times, Jo-Ann, when you feel as though I put a lot of pressure on you to meet deadlines (transferring). It's probably frustrating for you (peeking). I know that deadlines are frustrating for me." Brainstorm about the pressures on you and the implication of missing deadlines (exposing).

Next, share some of the assets, strengths, and resources that you have observed in Jo-Ann. "Well, Jo-Ann, you are one of the most talented typists I have ever seen. And your work is flawless. You are a real asset to the company."

Now, convey your new expectations. "Jo-Ann, I feel you're the kind of person who can take charge of the situation and meet the deadlines. You've done it many, many times. I will work extra hard myself to give you more time to complete the typing on projects. By using our combined skills and understanding, together we can do it."

Now comes the very important part. It is vital that you recognize Jo-Ann the next few times she successfully reaches her deadline and notice her achievements. You will be developing a claim-to-fame and a new asset—all because of your positive expectations. Jo-Ann becomes a winner!

How could you make use of expectation altering in your organization?

_____

_____

_____

Approach #24: Changing Spotlights

Changing spotlights involves putting the "spotlight" on a previously overlooked teammate.

A teacher's expectations influence student performance. A psychologist's expectations influence client outcome. A doctor's prognosis influences the patient's progress. And a leader's expectations influence the members' losing or winning feelings and their resultant performance.

When a member asks, "What does the leadership of this organization think of me?" one of the ways of answering the question is to assess how much responsibility the leadership has given to the person. It is indeed a fact that the toughest challenges are often given to the same people. Positive expectations, then, are usually communicated to only a few. Some get the winning feeling over and over again, while others never experience the respect.

Changing spotlights involves communicating positive expectations by taking a risk and giving the challenging job to a previously overlooked member. What a way to communicate "I believe in you!"

A new territory opens up in a small southern-based insurance company. The sales manager has to decide who will be given the opportunity to sell in the area. In making his decision, he realizes that he has always overlooked giving Charlie additional responsibilities, which is a message to Charlie that the sales manager does not have a lot of faith in him.

The sales manager takes a risk and changes spotlights. He calls Charlie in and shares with Charlie his newfound confidence (expectation alteration.) "Charlie, I'd like to give you a real challenge because I feel you have the potential to make it big in that region. I'm handing over to you the responsibilities there. Let's see you go out and sign them up. I'm here to support you with any additional training that you need."

Dumbfounded at first, Charlie is soon on a high. Somebody finally believes in him. He immediately goes out and buys himself a new suit, which perhaps reflects his newfound self-image. Charlie catches the winning feeling when his leader puts the spotlight on him.

Who could use a little more spotlighting? How could you give this person the winning feeling by spotlighting him or her?

_____

_____

_____

7

CONFRONT WITH CLASS: PICKING PEOPLE UP WITHOUT STOOPING DOWN

The word *confrontation* in itself generates a variety of emotional reactions in people. To some, confrontation elicits reminders of past encounters with bosses. To others, confrontation invites positive feelings of past victories over opponents, the IRS, or nasty neighbors. None of these views, neither from the victim's nor the victor's perspective, is relevant to this chapter. An entirely new view of confronting your employees, your children, your parents, or you team will be used here. The term applied to this new view is *classy confrontation.*

A classy confrontation is one in which the leader confronts someone for the purpose of building (like an education class). The leader wants to educate rather than defeat. Classy confrontations are designed to create a positive, healthy balance that is best for everyone involved. Learn to feel comfortable with and even enjoy the concept of confrontation. Confrontation, like asset focusing in Chapter 4, involves building people.

Unfortunately, confrontation has been associated with "gut-level talk," screaming, or on-the-spot firings. In some instances, the confronter explodes at the victim in an attempt to destroy or retaliate publicly or privately. The victim naturally becomes defensive and retaliates either directly or passive-aggressively to avoid being wiped out personally. In most cases, the defensiveness results in a message being distorted because of high emotional interchange, as in the following examples:

Confronter says	*Confrontee hears*
"You and I must have a face-to-face talk."	"I'm going to talk and you're going to listen."
"I'm going to level with you."	"I'm going to level you."
"I'm going to call it as I see it."	"You're in trouble."
"You just better cooperate."	"Cooperate means she tells me what to do and then I must do it."

In each instance, the confronter's words interfere with open communication and set the stage for anxious defensiveness. All of these confrontations lack class. They are not designed to build, but rather to frighten or to release anger. Consider a few of the different goals or motives of destructive versus classy confrontation:

Destructive reasons to confront	*Classy confrontations*
Trapping the other person	*Gathering* the facts
Assuming guilty until proven innocent	*Openness* to the confrontee's view
Gaining one-upmanship	*Balancing* the needs of all members
Releasing one's anger	*Educating* the person to more appropriate behavior

Destructive reasons to confront	Classy confrontations
Instilling fear	*Informing* the person why his or her behavior was unacceptable
Showing the other person who's boss. (A person who has to do things just to show who's boss isn't the boss.)	*Building* the person to change behaviors in the future

Remember, confrontation has received bad press in the past because it traditionally has been associated with having a destructive intent. Classy confrontation is designed to create a positive, healthy balance that is best for everyone. Classy confrontation builds, educates, and informs. Confrontation can be an additional leadership tool if it is given with respect for both the other person and oneself (picking people up without stooping down). Confrontation is built on the principle that dealing with a problem is almost always more effective than allowing the problem to continue.

When is action called for? A man who is living with symptoms of a disease each day feels that the symptoms are becoming more pronounced. He is too anxious to go to the doctor for fear of hearing the worst. He doesn't realize that perhaps the problem could be treated or maybe he has no problem at all and is experiencing unnecessary tension.

The biggest problem that the person experiences is the anxiety created by not knowing. His decision to avoid action on the problem drains his psychic energies. Action in this case is clearly called for because dealing with a problem is almost always more effective than allowing the problem to continue. Going to the doctor, like confronting yourself when you feel ill-at-ease, is a positive action that gathers the facts, educates, informs, and builds from that point.

Many unfortunate consequences can result when a leader avoids dealing with a problem. The leader forfeits an opportunity to help someone and creates an atmosphere that may affect overall morale. When the leader avoids the inevitable, he or she experiences frustration, anxiety, and possible loss of self-esteem.

Negative Consequences of Avoiding Confrontation

Forfeiting the Opportunity to Help Another Person

The important responsibility that a leader has to build people was stressed in Chapter 4. The point was made that you don't build by tearing down. It might be added that a leader doesn't build by allowing unproductive, unmotivated, or irresponsible behavior to continue. Confrontation is a form of assistance. Remember:

- The unproductive person is not fulfilled and needs assistance.

- The irresponsible, constantly late person is not motivated enough to be on time and needs assistance.

- The person who resists change in a growing organization is threatened and needs assistance.

- The person who is in a capacity above his or her potential is not eager to go to work in the morning, is tense, and needs assistance.

- The volunteer who is responsible for reaching certain campaign goals and is falling far short doesn't want to constantly make excuses and needs assistance.

Assistance from a motivating leader is called *classy confrontation.* When a leader avoids confronting, he or she surrenders the opportunity to help the other person learn some new ideas that could be beneficial over a lifetime.

For example, a classy confrontation can help an otherwise competent person who has only one problem, for example, poor hygiene habits, to become a more productive person. Wouldn't you want to be confronted in this instance?

A classy confrontation can stimulate a rude waiter or waitress to change his or her behavior, which could potentially generate many more tips. Wouldn't you want to experience a classy confrontation if you were that waiter or waitress? Remember, we are not talking about a destructive confrontation, but a classy one!

One consequence of avoiding a confrontation when it is indicated is that the opportunity to help another person is forfeited. A second consequence of avoiding a confrontation can be seen in the other teammates.

Loss of Respect for Leadership or Low Morale*

One thing is clear: the members of a team see irresponsibility in one of their co-workers even before the leader does—and they are watching for the response of leadership. When leadership avoids confrontation, the other more responsible members cannot help but notice, which is reflected in the following typical comments: "Why should we work so hard if she can come in late." "I wouldn't put up with that if I were the boss." "It just makes more work for us when he doesn't pull his fair share."

A classy confrontation is one that is designed to create a positive, healthy balance that is best for everyone involved. When a member of the team isn't pulling his or her fair share, an imbalance exists, and everyone else is affected. Unless the leader is willing to give everyone else the same leeway, the imbalance will affect the team's morale. The irresponsible party in a classy confrontation is simply being asked to give what is expected—no more, no less. The leader has not only the right but the respon-

---

* Obviously, any area dealing with discipline or confrontation in this book needs to be tailored to be consistent with specific union contracts and specific ethical practices of any organization.

sibility to confront. Avoiding the helpful confrontation may result in loss of respect for leadership and lowered morale. Remember, dealing with a problem is almost always better than allowing the problem to continue.

Personal Problems

A third consequence of avoiding a confrontation has a direct impact on the leader's emotional life. Timid leaders may find themselves experiencing any of the following symptoms:

1. *Passive-aggressiveness:* Passive-aggressive behavior is seen in people who have difficulty expressing feelings such as anger, hurt, and resentment. They hold these feelings in and show an outward facade that conveys the opposite. They may smile and say, "No, there's no problem." The leader who is upset but avoids confrontation denies the need for a confrontation and exhibits his or her anger in passive ways, such as refusing to talk, putting obstacles in the way, and indirectly getting back at the target person. Passive-aggressiveness is seen in almost any relationship where a timid person feels afraid to confront.

2. *Anxiety:* Another symptom often observed in leaders who avoid confrontation is an anxiety characterized by feelings of tension, worries over an impending catastrophe, loss of sleep over what could happen the next day, or a continued reliving of the previous day and how the situation was handled. The anxious leader has difficulty taking a stance as well as making decisions.

3. *Displaced hostility:* When a leader avoids a confrontation, the resentment held in sometimes is redirected toward an alternate target person. The computer shop manager who avoids confronting his irresponsible employees may lash out at his wife or children at home. The anger is displaced onto a scapegoat or a

safer person. The tension in the organization is taken home, which produces a tense home life.

4. *Escapism:* The leader who avoids a confrontation may resort to extreme forms of avoidance and denial by escaping into gambling, drugs, alcohol, daydreaming, or excessive sleep. These symptoms could have been avoided if the leader had taken charge and confronted at the appropriate time. Dealing with a problem is almost always easier than allowing a problem to continue.

Confronting with Class: Picking People Up Without Stooping Down

Confronting, if done with the motive to educate, is a positive and effective leadership tool. It is clear that avoiding a necessary confrontation has many negative consequences. The effectiveness of a confrontation depends on how it is done. Several approaches are provided in this chapter to help a leader set the stage up front to prevent problems before they occur and confront in a positive way to build the confrontee.

Four classy confrontation approaches are discussed:

- Speed limiting
- Asserting
- Disciplining
- De-hiring

Confronting with class is especially relevant for the following challenges:

1. Irresponsibility
2. Discipline problems
3. First conference as a new leader

4. Lateness

5. Lying

6. Poor work performance

7. Negativism

8. Firing

9. Creating mutual expectations

10. Dealing with defensiveness

Approach #25: Speed Limiting

Speed limiting is a preventive technique that a leader uses to define limits ahead of time for the purpose of maximizing the freedom of the total team. Setting speed limits also reduces anxiety by clarifying rights, responsibilities, and roles and aligning expectations.

Imagine a small township police department operating without any stated laws. No speed limit signs are posted publicly, even though the chief of police has a limit in mind. The chief tells the police officers to stop people who are going too fast. A person driving through town at 60 miles an hour is apprehended and brought to the chief.

"But I didn't see any speed limit signs, Chief, and I just assumed that there were no limits," says the driver. "Don't be so stupid," the chief replies. "Common sense tells you that when you are in a town you don't speed." "That's common sense to you," responds the driver, "but common sense to me is that if there are no other cars on the road, no people walking down the streets, and no speed limit signs posted and I'm late for a meeting, I go as fast as is reasonable." "But what you were doing can certainly not be called reasonable," the chief answers "But with respect, Chief," says the driver, "what is reasonable? Where is the guideline? How can I be in violation of a rule that doesn't exist?" The chief replies, "You should have known better."

The chief's failure to post speed limits is an injustice to the healthy citizens who want to comply but didn't know what to comply with. Lack of speed limits produces anxiety among the membership who wonder, "How fast can I go here?" "Am I going too fast or not fast enough?" Speed limits reduce anxiety by providing guidelines for acceptable and unacceptable behavior. Speed limiting is a leadership approach designed to achieve two results:

1. To define limits to bring maximum freedom to the total membership
2. To reduce anxiety by providing guidelines that create mutual expectations

Speed Limiting Gives Maximum Freedom to the Total Membership

Speed limiting has the effect of expanding freedom rather than constricting it. If a meeting of the total membership is to begin promptly at nine o'clock and one out of ten members arrives late, which holds up the other nine, 90 percent of the membership loses freedom due to lost time.

When the printing department, one out of five departments in the organization, does not meet its deadline for promotional materials, the other 80 percent of the organization loses some of its freedom to act because of its dependency on that one cog in the wheel.

If one member of the tour bus takes too much time at a particular sight, the whole group loses its freedom and right to see the next sight.

Speed limits are created to maximize the freedoms of the total team.

Speed Limiting Reduces Anxiety by Providing Guidelines that Create Mutual Expectations

Without direction, people on teams have to guess what is expected. This guessing produces haphazard behaviors. In some instances, people may feel that they are acting consistently with leadership's expectations only to find themselves confronted at some later point for poor performance.

A good friend of mine was appointed superintendent of schools in a large northeastern U.S. city. The new leader was a teacher-oriented manager who believed that teachers were the very backbone of the school and, consequently, should play a major role in educational decisions. The new superintendent saw the role of the school principals as encouragers to their faculty members.

The youthful superintendent's management position was in direct contradiction to his predecessor's philosophy. The previous leader believed that teachers should be monitored closely in order to weed out incompetence. These changes in expectations from the top literally led to a new view of what constituted an effective performance. Imagine that you are a school principal and experience the confusion over establishing job priorities.

The superintendent related the following story. "Shortly after I took over my new position, a school principal asked for a meeting with me. The principal came to tell me, quite proudly, that he had accumulated enough facts on a few of his teachers to take action against them for the purpose of having them removed. The principal went on to say that he had spent many hours gathering information to prove these teachers incompetent." The superintendent went on, "And while I'm not naive to the fact that in teaching, as in all professions, there are incompetent people, spending 50 percent of one's important time as a principal to look for incompetence isn't justified when there are so many more important things to do."

The principal was not a bad person; he was simply doing his job consistent with what he thought was expected of him. The problem was not a complex one. The principal just needed to know what new expectations were being placed on him.

When the superintendent wisely took some time to develop and state his management philosophy to the school principals, he initiated structure by listing his expectations and his view of an acceptable performance. His stated philosophy gave the principals the frame of reference they needed.

Do your people know exactly what is expected of them? Does your team know what is acceptable and what is unacceptable performance? Do your team members know very clearly and very specifically what they are responsible for? Are your employees fully aware of the authority they have when you are and are not present? Do you teammates know what kinds of decisions they can make?

While sitting with the owner of a restaurant in Edmonton, Alberta, both of us overheard a customer at the next table complain about the excessive amount of gristle in her steak. The waitress, speechless for a moment and fully aware of her boss at the next table, replied, "Sorry, I hope it's better next time." Having made the decision not to take the meat back and thus save the restaurant money, she turned to her boss, Frank, in anticipation of his approval of her decision.

Frank excused himself from our table and politely advised the waitress to very graciously order the customer a new steak.

As Frank returned to the table where I was seated, he told me something that has always stuck with me. "You can't blame the waitress for her decision not to take the food back," the highly successful restaurateur concluded. "It's my fault. As I think of it, I've never really put into words to my waiters and waitresses that my prime concern is satisfied customers." He thoughtfully continued, "The waitress thought she was making the decision I wanted her to make. And I do believe, for the most part, that employees want to do what their manager wants. But not specifically spelling out to my people what I expect or want from them, not stating my needs, is like trying to hitchhike without putting your thumb up. I can't expect someone to pick me up if I don't tell them I need a lift. I can't expect my employees to reach into my head and make the decisions I want them to without stating my wants."

Frank and I took a few minutes and brainstormed a simple clear-cut management philosophy, a speed limiting plan that we called a problem prevention plan. Read Frank's plan and consider developing a problem prevention plan of your own to let your people know what you stand for and what is expected of them.

Problem Prevention Management Plan in Frank's Restaurant

1. I believe that above all else, customer satisfaction is the goal of our restaurant. As a waiter or waitress, constantly think to yourself, what does this customer need to be satisfied and to have a good experience while here?

2. I believe that the employees working here are as creative and important as the owner or manager. I welcome any ideas or suggestions for improvement that any employees have. I will reward your ideas if we use them. Even if they aren't used, I would be thrilled to hear them. After all, the waiters and waitresses are out there with the customers every day and know as much as anyone.

3. I value competence, excellence, promptness, and people with a desire to improve themselves. Thus, if any of you would like to learn more about the restaurant business, I will support opportunities for you to grow by becoming more involved in the business or getting additional training in bookkeeping, cooking, and so on. Just let me know of your interests. With good employees, our business will expand, which in turn will provide expanded opportunities for everyone who chooses to stay with us.

4. Our restaurant faces a lot of pressures. As the owner, I have made investments of time, money, and energy

to build up the business. I made decisions along the way to hire certain employees who I believed would best help the business to succeed. For the most part, I am pleased with employee performance. At times, however, employee behavior will make me act to get our restaurant back on course. The following are problems to me:

a. When employees are late, it puts pressure on the other teammates to work extra hard. This is unfair, and, therefore, no lateness can be tolerated. If an unexpected problem occurs, it is vital that you call us immediately so that we can replace you during that day. If an employee is late once without calling in, I will meet with the person to remind him or her. The second lateness will be followed by two days off work. A third lateness will result in dismissal. I feel that it is reasonable to expect a phone call from a late employee.

b. Another behavior that simply can't be tolerated in a restaurant that offers a relaxing dining experience is a negative attitude with customers or with other employees. I have implemented a customer evaluation card to help us evaluate ourselves and our services. This is for your benefit, not mine. This will provide you with feedback about how people view you and is, I believe, an excellent tool for a person who wants to become the best he or she can. If I hear a complaint, I will share it with you. If I begin to hear complaints regularly, for instance, more than three in one week, I will schedule a meeting with you and will ask you to take additional customer relations training. A good attitude by everyone helps everyone else. Let's strive to avoid problems of negative attitudes.

5. My door is always open to any of you when you have a problem or a need. I hope that your door will be open for me as well when I need you to stay a little

later when an unexpected big party arrives, for example. Let's work together. Let's avoiding small talk and negative thinking. Let's encourage each other, and we will have a pleasant experience together. Thank you.

Frank shared these ideas at every meeting with his employees. He posted his philosophy at various locations around the restaurant as well. Because of his little extra effort, he created a harmony of expectations. He reduced many employee problems by helping his employees know what he expected of them and what he defined a good job to be.

Advantages of Creating Speed Limits with the Involvement of the Total Membership

Since most of the members benefit from a problem prevention plan or a speed limit, more and more organizations create the plan with everyone involved. Based on the Cahn principle, "people need to be involved with decisions that affect their lives." Speed limits can be developed most effectively by those who are affected by the limits.

As a consultant to an upper New York state school district, we discussed how some of the problems of classroom disruptiveness could be avoided.

"It involves only two or three percent of our kids here," the high school principal commented. "The balance of our kids want to learn."

"Well, it sounds like you have a natural answer here," I replied. "If 98 percent of your students want an organized classroom, why not let them play a role in developing the rules that affect their lives? Instead of the administration shoving rules down the throats of everyone from their perspective, why not have rules established by the total student body. It will be a lesson in democracy as well as a responsibility-building experience, and it comes from them, not you."

Dialogues took place in all of the classrooms, and the students created their own code of acceptable behavior and consequences of violation. The administration was totally satisfied, and 98 percent of the students gained more freedom through setting their own speed limits.

Leadership is quite simple if the leader is sure that the people know the answers to four questions:

- What am I responsible for?
- What kind of authority do I have?
- What kind of decisions can I make?
- What does my job entail?

How can you make use of the first approach to classy confrontation: speed limiting?

_____

_____

_____

Approach #26: Asserting

Asserting occurs when the leader confronts a teammate who violates the speed limits. Assertive leadership is a healthy balance between timid leadership and aggressive leadership.

When someone stands on your foot, you can continue to allow the person to dig in while you seethe inside (timid); you can push the person away, throw him or her to the ground, and tread on his or her face (aggressive); or you can say, "take your foot off of my foot" (assertive).

When someone violates the speed limits of your organization, you can ignore the infringement (timid), you can severely punish the person (aggressive), or you can act appropriately to educate, inform, and discipline to build (assert).

Your Perfect Right by Robert Alberti and Michael Emmons (1982) was, in my estimation, the first important writing on the topic of assertiveness, and today it is still one of the most practiced philosophies. Alberti and Emmons classified behavior as timid, assertive, and aggressive and later as non-assertive, assertive, and aggressive.

Asserting is finding the balance between timidity and aggressiveness.

"I literally feared walking into my own business," the former owner of a small music shop told me. "My young employees held me hostage in my own store. I was too frightened to ask them to do even routine chores like unloading a shipment of new cassettes. So I did them myself. If I saw the cashier loafing while there was a line of customers waiting to be checked out, I would run over to the register and personally check each customer out. Then, at the end of the day, I'd be angry at myself for not showing my people who was boss. Here I was, the owner, the one who made the financial investment in the business in the first place, and I felt like the low man on the totem pole."

The prematurely graying former entrepreneur continued, "Then one day it happened—the most embarrassing moment of my life. I was running back and forth in the store like a miner in a landslide while two of my employees were plugged into headsets, doing their own thing, I guess. A customer looked at me and said, 'I've never in my life seen a circus like this place. You seem to be the only one who does any work around here. In fact, I've been in here a number of times, and every time it's the same story. You are working five times as hard as all those other clowns put together. Let me do you a favor,' the customer confided. 'I'd like to talk to your manager and tell him what goes on when he's not around and also tell him that if he should ever decide to let you go, I'd hire you immediately. You see, I own the book store in the downtown mall and could sure use someone like you. What time will your manager be in?'"

"Scared to admit that I was supposed to be the ring-leader and was responsible for all of this chaos," the frustrated manager went on, "I lied to the helpful gentle-man and said that the manager was on vacation. He left. All boiled up, I immediately closed the shop and took my people to the woodshed. Giving way to my month of pent up anger, I exploded like Vesuvius and fired two of my three people on the spot. And even though I enjoyed the business of selling records, within three months I closed up shop and went to work for someone else, where I wouldn't have to deal with people problems. You see," the compromised man concluded, "I'm not the kind of person who is cut out to be a manager of people."

The record store manager had irresponsible employ-ees, but they were not quite as irresponsible as their manager was! The employees' jobs included unloading records and cashing people out; they failed. The manager's job included showing his employees what their jobs were, motivating them to achieve those goals, rewarding them when they did, and confronting them when they didn't. The manager failed as well.

The manager discouraged his employees by not giv-ing them direction. Timid managers run away from em-ployee problems and wish or pray that when they come to work the next day, the problems will have magically disappeared; they rarely do. Perhaps you'd like to take a minute to think about a few instances when you have been timid.

Some leaders, on the other hand, are *aggressive*. While the timid leader's philosophy of life is "die and let live," the aggressive leader believes "live and let die." Alberti and Emmons write:

> The person who carries a desire for self-expression to the extreme of aggressive behavior accomplishes goals at the expense of others. Although frequently self-enhancing and expression of feelings in the situ-ation, aggressive behavior hurts other people in the process by making choices for them and by minimiz-ing their worth.

Aggressive behavior commonly results in a put-down of the receiver. Rights denied, the receiver feels hurt, defensive and humiliated. His or her goals in the situation, of course, are not achieved. Aggressive behavior may achieve the sender's goals, but may also generate bitterness and frustration which may later return as vengeance (Alberti and Emmons, 1982).

The aggressive leader wants not only a fair share, but more than what is reasonable, or two eyes for an eye and two teeth for a tooth. Actions of aggressive leaders reflect not only the demand for justice, but also retaliation, greed, and one-upmanship.

Reflect on some examples when you may have seen the line between assertiveness and aggressiveness crossed.

Assertive leadership is a balance between timid and aggressive leadership. Contrast the three styles of leadership shown on page 153.

Identify a few instances where you are currently asserting yourself appropriately.

Make a plan to become assertive in those circumstances when you have previously responded in either a timid or aggressive fashion.

Timid	Assertive	Aggressive
Die and let live.	Live and let live.	Live and let die.
I'll tolerate violation of the speed limits in the membership. Maybe someday they'll appreciate me.	I'm not obsessed with looking for violations. Most of my energies are spent on spotting what's right. However, when a violation occurs, I will deal with it constructively to build the person. I will apply the appropriate discipline that is called for. Then we will start over again fresh.	I'll make the punishment so severe that no one will ever dare break a rule. I'll show them.
Avoidance, passive-aggressiveness, martyrism	Private, asserting, rational thinking, active openness	Sarcasm, publicly disgracing, put-downs

Approach #27: Disciplining

Disciplining with class is a specific five-step process used by the assertive, encouraging leader to deal with offenders of the team's speed limits.

By using speed limiting and a positive prevention plan, a leader can create conditions that will lower the need for classy confrontations. When problems do occur, the next step is to assess *if* and *when* assertiveness is appropriate. If the leader concludes that it is time to act, the specific approach is all-important. In this encouraging approach to disciplining, a very specific process to deal assertively is described. The leader, of course, tailors wisdom and discretion to the unique circumstances of the situation.

Disciplining with class is a five-step process to deal with offenders of the team's speed limits. The five steps are

1. Gathering the facts

2. Setting discipline conference goals prior to the meeting

3. Scheduling the discipline conference

4. Using a ten-step approach to confront with class during the conference

5. Following up after the conference

Gathering the Facts

Some leaders find themselves apologizing after the fact because they forgot the simple rule of justice: People are innocent until proven guilty. More often than not, leadership lacks the full story at the onset of a crisis and responds impulsively to what someone said. Before scheduling the conference, it is vital for the leader to ask, "Is the probability strong that there was a violation of the speed limits and that it is necessary to confront?" If the answer is yes, then it is the appropriate time to establish goals for the conference (Step 2).

Setting Discipline Conference Goals Prior to the Meeting

Leaders frequently create problems for themselves because they fail to establish their goals before actual discipline meetings. Wandering through this important session without a plan guarantees that the goals will not be reached. The goals govern the meeting, and the leader should never stray from them.

Consider, for example, the goals that a motivating leader might establish with Charlie, a salesman who has filed expense reports stating that he called on certain accounts. His manager, however, has received calls from the accounts indicating that Charlie never visited them.

Goals for Conference with Charlie

1. Inform Charlie that I am aware of his actions.

2. Apply appropriate discipline as stated in the speed limits and positive prevention plan for violation of policy.

3. State what will constitute acceptable behavior in the future.

4. Reestablish a positive working relationship with Charlie and motivate him.

The leader has gathered the facts and established the goals for the discipline conference. He or she is now ready to schedule the conference (Step 3).

Scheduling the Discipline Conference

The ideal discipline conference achieves the goals and at the same time actually builds the violating member. To maximize the effectiveness of the conference, it is important to create conditions that allow the confronted person to arrive with as open and non-defensive an attitude as possible.

A few suggestions for achieving the best atmosphere for the conference include:

1. Confront as soon as you have gathered the facts and established the goals for the meeting. The longer the time between the violation and the discipline, the less effective the discipline.

2. Avoid anxiety-producing statements like "I'll see you in my office after work today," which has the person on edge all day. Instead, try to make the time between the meeting and the announcement as short as possible.

3. Give the person an idea of what issue the conference will address. "Charlie, I'd like to talk with you as soon as possible about some of your expense reports so that we can straighten the matter out."

The leader has now gathered the facts, set the conference goals, and scheduled the conference. He or she is now ready for the most delicate moment a leader faces—the discipline conference.

Ten Steps to Confront with Class During the Conference

The motivating leader maximizes the effectiveness of the conference by employing ten steps to confront with class:

1. Start the conference on a positive note. Review Chapter 4 for ways to identify some of the person's assets, strengths, or resources.

    "Charlie, first of all I'd like to say to you what I've often said before. You really are a great salesman. You know how to talk with people. Dale Carnegie could have learned some things from you. And you are a real asset to this company. We need you."

2. Point out the problem specifically (avoid anger, name calling, etc.).

   "It's because of your talent which I feel isn't being used to its fullest potential that I called you in here today. When your sales drop, the company sales drop. Very frankly, Charlie, I had three calls in the last two weeks from different accounts saying that you didn't call on them. Yet I have your expense reports showing that you made these calls."

3. Encourage the person to speak, and listen for the person's view, feelings, and defenses (Chapter 3).

   "Can you tell me a little more about this, Charlie?"

   Note here that defensive people must defend. The motivating leader does not let defensive anger or revenge cloud the focus of the goals of the conference. Some typical defensive reactions might include:

The violator's defense	*The motivating leader's reaction*
"You have the wrong story, boss."	Be open to hearing the other side of the story.
"I needed the money." (pity me)	Understand the difficult economic times he or she faces, but keep the goals in mind.
"I'm sorry."	"Charlie, it's encouraging to hear that you recognize that you made a mistake. That's great news for our working relationship in the future." (keep goals in mind)
"None of the other people get disciplined," or "I'm the best, and I deserve a little more." (excusing, blaming)	Understand. "It doesn't seem fair to you, but you know the rules, Charlie, and you violated one of them."

4. Convey your understanding and respect for the employee's view and feelings (Chapter 3). (*"You feel..."*)

5. Present your view and why the employee's actions present a problem to the organization.

    "I filed a report to my boss about the number of calls our salespeople made last week. My report is now inaccurate. Also, the accounts are angry that they are not being serviced because of your actions, Charlie."

6. Indicate the discipline, along with a clear understanding of what the discipline will be if the violation occurs again.

7. Share very clearly the desirable behavior you now expect.

8. Point out again the specific assets, strengths, and resources the individual has.

9. Provide hope and confidence in the employee's ability to contribute to the team. Mark a new beginning.

10. Thank the employee for his or her time.

The motivating leader controls the conference by using the ten steps to confronting with class and is now ready for the last phase of the discipline process, the follow-up.

Follow Up the Discipline Conference

Charlie's manager was sensitive to any improved behavior in the new Charlie. He made it a point to be the first to say, "Good job! Your work sure is an asset to our company. I'm proud of you, Charlie."

An assertive, encouraging leader who confronts with class can turn even the most troublesome people into producers by using the five phases of effective discipline:

1. Gather the facts

2. Set discipline conference goals prior to the meeting

3. Schedule the discipline conference

4. Use the ten-step approach to confront with class during the conference

5. Follow up after the conference

While it is fresh in your mind, make a few notes to help you remember the most important aspects of disciplining.

Approach #28: De-hiring

De-hiring is the process of breaking the ties with a teammate who has continuously violated the rules of the team's speed limits and who has not responded positively to other motivational approaches.

De-hiring is a term developed by author Donald Scoleri. It is based on the realistic fact that there are times when the team's needs and a team member's needs are not compatible. Let's assume that the leader has made reasonable attempts to understand (Chapter 3), to build (Chapter 4), and to give meaning (Chapter 5) and concludes that the relationship is good for neither party. When a member's needs are not being met, he or she looks for alternatives, thus de-hiring the team. This happens every day. There are also times when the team's needs are not being met by an individual, and thus the leader needs to de-hire. The experience of a person de-hiring the team or the team de-hiring an individual can be anything from painful to a relief. How the de-hiring is done makes the vital difference.

Facts to Remember When De-hiring

1. Chances are the person is neither happy nor fulfilled on the team.

2. Chances are the person senses that the event is inevitable and is going to occur sometime soon.

3. Chances are the person subconsciously wants out anyway.

4. Chances are he or she has had a discipline conference.

5. Chances are the member is having social problems with his or her teammates.

The motivating leader who de-hires with class is well aware that the needs of neither the individual nor the team are being met. This demands a response of assertiveness on the leader's part. The leader is also aware that the person is probably dissatisfied and unfulfilled in the current situation.

The motivating leader needs to keep a few things in mind when de-hiring:

• I have communicated to this person a sincere analysis of his or her assets and resources and even given some advice as to where he or she more effectively fits in the organization.

• I have not destroyed this person out of my own anger or need for retaliation.

• In cases where it is relevant, I have pointed out how the economy of the company or other reasons for cutbacks necessitated the decision, rather than this person's own worth.

• While this decision may temporarily appear to be to this person's disadvantage, it may, in the long haul, turn out to be in his or her best interest.

If you are currently in the process of de-hiring, how can you make use of any of these approaches?

_____

_____

_____

Ten Crucial Things to Remember and Ten Practical Things to Do from Chapter 7

1. **Remember:** Dealing with a problem is almost always better than allowing the problem to continue, so...

   Do: Become determined to address those problems that monopolize your time and thoughts. But first, make sure that:

   1. Your expectations are clearly stated.
   2. You are prepared to confront based on the process of confronting with encouragement discussed in this chapter.

2. **Remember:** Two ineffective styles of leadership that produce disharmony are timidity, in which confrontation is avoided, and aggressiveness, in which the leader creates unnecessary confrontation, so...

   Do: Find the balance between the timid and the aggressive style. Be an assertive, encouraging leader. Make it crystal clear to your people that you will confront when there is a violation of rules and expectations. By the same token, you are not lurking over their shoulders just waiting to spring on them.

3. **Remember:** Many problems are related to the simple fact that the leader has not clarified what the roles, responsibilities, and rights of the membership are, so...

   Do: Ask yourself if your people know the answer to the following four questions:

   1. What am I responsible for?
   2. What kind of authority do I have?
   3. What sort of decisions can I make?
   4. What does my job entail?

4. **Remember:** You and your team need to have a mutual understanding of what their jobs entail and what is acceptable and unacceptable behavior, so...

Do: Over the next few weeks, develop your philosophy or problem prevention plan, which sets the speed limits. This plan will:

1. Give guidelines or standards
2. Reduce anxiety
3. Demonstrate that everyone is bound by the same rules
4. Enable your people to see the consequences of violating the rules
5. Give you peace of mind
6. Maximize freedom

5. **Remember:** When you must meet with a specific person to confront due to lack of performance or a violation of the speed limits, there are two ways of proceeding: the destructive way and the constructive way, so...

   Do: Become familiar with the five-phase process of discipline:

   1. Gather the facts
   2. Set conference goals
   3. Schedule the meeting
   4. Use the ten steps to confront with class
   5. Follow up

   By using these five phases, you can improve your chances of having a constructive discipline conference to steer the person back on track.

6. **Remember:** Unless you have specific constructive goals for your meeting, you have no direction and no target, and you may wander aimlessly in this important encounter, so...

   Do: Know exactly what you want to achieve in your meeting. Make sure that the conference is not designed to simply enhance your own ego or release your anger or revenge. A constructive conference is designed to develop more appropriate and productive behaviors or attitudes.

7. **Remember:** Assume that when you confront someone, he or she will naturally become defensive, so...
   Do: Be prepared to cope with defenses to your confrontations by being familiar with the leader reaction list to defenses on page 157.

8. **Remember:** An effective discipline conference deals with specific behaviors or attitudes (not personalities) and gives specific suggestions for improvement, so...
   Do: Make sure the person knows specifically why he or she is being disciplined as well as the specific behaviors that are expected in the future.

9. **Remember:** A positive beginning opens the person up to what is to follow. By ending your conference on a positive note, you invite the person back on the team, so...
   Do: Make the discipline conference mark a new beginning, with no grudges held.

10. **Remember:** If a person is dissatisfied, he or she leaves or de-hires the team. If the team is dissatisfied, it de-hires the person. De-hiring does not have to be a destructive experience done without class, so...
    Do: Build the individual by identifying those assets that you see in him or her, and add some suggestions as to how he or she might be more fulfilled.

8

INSPIRE YOUR TEAM TO FIND A WAY

The ultimate test of what a leader is really made of is not seen during the sunny times, when prosperity allows wasted resources to go unnoticed. The supreme test of a leader's substance comes when the dark clouds descend upon the team and every voice is too busy singing songs of doom to build an ark. It is in these difficult times that one or two people emerge to face the rain head on and make plans for the future, knowing that they have the resources to make the sun come out tomorrow. These human catalysts are the opti-realistic leaders. This chapter takes a microscopic view of the mental workings of these rare individuals who make the difference in the success of a team.

The Opti-realistic Leader

Tough times in an organization are as inevitable as rain. Doomsday leaders can be observed helplessly responding to a crisis like a building looking at the swinging construction ball, awaiting demise. Other pessimistic leaders disappear during a storm and aren't heard from again until the sun comes out. Quixotic leaders, on the other hand, act as if it weren't raining and then get drenched because of their refusal to face reality.

The doomsday and pessimistic leaders breed a "what's the use" philosophy among the membership. When people function based on the belief that there are no answers, they make no attempt to seek them. The over-idealistic leader, on the other hand, doesn't encourage a search for solutions to problems because he or she doesn't acknowledge the problems. Hence, the over-idealistic leader's style breeds distrust or disrespect, because he or she is viewed as either dishonest or naive.

And then there emerges the one leader in ten—the person who sees the problem, faces it clearly and realistically, and communicates an optimism that says, "We can find a solution." This person, the opti-realistic leader, is one of the first people contacted by top leadership for help during a crisis. This leader is not a game player. He or she is a solid citizen, solid with strength and with hope, and a stranger to excuse making. It is the opti-realistic leader who has buildings and streets that bear his or her name.

What separates the opti-realistic leader from the other 90 percent? First of all, it is an attitude and a strong conviction to see reality "as it is"—undeluded by personal needs. Second, the opti-realistic leader is buoyed by a stubborn underlying belief that there are solutions to the problems that the team faces. Thus, the opti-realistic leader creates a "find-a-way" atmosphere on the team.

Six second-gearing approaches are presented in this chapter:

- Jonas Salking
- Environmental engineering
- Talking it up
- Sweet surrendering

- Rational leading
- Opti-realistic leading

By using these approaches, the opti-realistic leader can ignite the "find-a-way" energies of the membership to solve:

1. Frustration

2. Burnout

3. Cynicism

4. Lack of motivation

5. Stagnation

Approach #29: Jonas Salking

Jonas Salking occurs when the leader inspires the team to operate based on the conviction that problems have solutions.

If you think of it, it was only a few decades ago when there were no washing machines, airplanes, buses, satellites, geodesic domes, fast-food restaurants, open-heart surgery, Trivial Pursuit, multi-media computers, and almost everything else that you see around you. If those few decades ago the world had been composed of only pessimists, none of these things would exist today!

These modern-day conveniences exist only because of the optimists who could see beyond what their eyes saw. Perhaps the best example is Jonas Salk, who discovered the vaccine that cured polio. Suppose Salk had been a pessimist and had given up on his journey. Suppose he had listened to the cynics of the day and turned his energies elsewhere, like writing about despair and hopelessness in life. Fortunately for the world, he didn't. Salk argued that we should not be limited in our visions of the future by our experiences of the past.

"Jonas Salking" is a leadership approach designed to create the feeling in the membership that "our problems do have solutions." This mental attitude is orchestrated by a "we can find a way" leadership attitude that helps push the minds of the membership one step further. A frustrated membership sees no options. As philosopher Baruch Spinoza wrote, "For as long as a person believes a task to be impossible, for that exact period of time no progress is possible." But the hour, the minute, the second that someone inspires others to find the solution, that is the moment that the membership moves toward fulfillment. Henry Ford said, "Believe you can or believe you can't, either way you'll be correct."

More conservatively, those who are inspired by a leader to look for the answer to a challenge may or may not find it, while those who do not look at all certainly will not find it. "Maybes" offer more possibilities than "nos," don't they?

Jonas Salking can be achieved in a variety of ways. One possible approach is as follows:

1. The leader identifies past examples in which everyone on the team was ready to give up, when someone discovered a solution, and the membership solved its problem.

2. The leader encourages everyone to relax and to operate out of the assumption that somewhere in the unlimited universe of their collective minds a solution exists.

3. The membership brainstorms about possible solutions in an atmosphere of total, unconditional acceptance.

4. Every attempt (risk) is noticed and recognized (especially if some of the membership laughs at a suggestion).

5. The leader responds enthusiastically to any progress. "We're getting closer. The answer is there, let's find it."

6. The team celebrates the progress. "Look at how far we have come tonight with your suggestions."

Identify three challenges that your team currently faces, and use Jonas Salking to inspire them.

_____

_____

_____

Approach #30: Environmental Engineering

Environmental engineering is the process of consciously engineering both the social and physical environments in positive ways in order to constantly give the team a lift.

It is generally accepted that people are products of their environments. I would like to add that environments are also products of people. Motivating leaders take responsibility for shaping the environment—the environment that is shaping the attitude of the people on the team.

Just as the air we breath in from our physical environment affects our physical health, our psychological environment affects our psychological health. An unstimulating, drab, or negative environment is unlikely to produce a find-a-way attitude. Motivating leaders build uplifting, positive environments by being environmental engineers. A leader can alter two factors:

1. People environment
2. Physical environment

Environmental Engineering: People Environment

To keep oneself in a find-a-way mode, it is crucial to avoid, as much as possible, people who are down on life. People's attitudes rub off, and the rule of social influence is that we tend to become like the people with whom we associate.

The motivating leader knows that I must surround myself with people who have the characteristics that I myself want to develop. If I want to learn Spanish, I am better off spending time in Spain than in Canada. If I want to quit smoking, I must surround myself with non-smokers. If I want to appreciate life, I must surround myself with people whose ideas on life are upbeat and inspirational.

A motivating leader also realizes the principle that you never seek advice from someone who has not achieved the things you want to achieve. Don't ask a depressed person for the meaning of life. Don't ask an angry person for his or her secret. Don't ask a bankrupt person how to invest.

In *Think Your Way to Success,* I suggest that the reader hire a board of positive consultants to help design his or her environment. Don't take on such an important challenge as designing your environment by yourself. As director of environmental engineering, you have the power not only to de-hire, but to hire people to assist you. So hire your own board of free advisors to be part of your super successfully stimulating environment.

The simplest task in the world is selecting the people who will be on your board of positive consultants. Identify at least five people based on the following qualifications: (1) You feel positive about yourself and life when you are with them. (2) You feel courageously willing to try new experiences and take new risks when you are with them. (3) You feel free to speak and share even your craziest new ideas in their presence. Take this important exercise to heart, and jot down the names of the people you have honored by your selections. In your environment, a positive friend is like a rare gem.

When you have established who you would like on your board of advisors, make a point of telling each of them that you have read a book on the importance of having positive consultants. Tell each person the three requirements for a person to be a positive advisor and that you have selected him or her for the position. Then ask each person to consider accepting a position on your advisory board, and express your confidence in the fact that acceptance involves nothing more than continuing to be himself or herself. Your comments will elate all of them. How would you feel if someone complimented you by saying that out of everyone he or she knows, you are one of the most positive influences on his or her life? After you share your news, you will rarely find any one of these people "down" in your presence.

Become determined to spend more time with each of your board members in the future. Make plans to see them and talk with them, even if on the telephone. When you consider the fact that people pay $90 to $125 an hour to talk with a psychiatrist or to listen to a motivational lecturer, friends who help a person feel positive are worth quite a bit. Don't neglect positive advisors, the richest sources of input.

The great news is that it doesn't even matter if you can't be near your board of advisors due to distance or timing. When facing a difficult decision or a challenging situation, recall your advisors' thinking by visualizing their reactions to the event. Imagine confronting each positive person with your situation, and picture each one's response and advice. The results of their advice will prove to be quite interesting, if not incredible. Most of your free advisors will probably agree on the best course of action for you! As director of environmental engineering for yourself, hire the most positive people you know and watch your positive self-image grow. Now, add an honorary board of advisors composed of the most inspirational thinkers in the world (Losoncy, 1982).

The first way to engineer your environment is to let your thinking be influenced by people's ideas that work. The second way to influence your environment is to alter its physical components.

Environmental Engineering: Physical Environment

A second-gearing environment is one that gives the team constant upbeat talk, reminds them to keep plugging away, and provides for the needs of relaxation, stimulation, mediation, and inspiration. Advertisers spend millions of dollars on jingles, phrases, colors, sights, and sounds to effectively influence buying habits. Why? Because it works. Creating a stimulating, find-a-way environment can work for an organization if the leader takes advantage of this multi-million dollar idea.

Many companies take their work force to a fine hotel for their training and development programs to get them away from the ho-hum everyday work atmosphere. They realize that if you want new ideas, you need new surroundings to stimulate the membership.

1. *Start an advertising campaign in your environment.* Imagine that you are the leader of a weight-loss group. Encourage the membership to build their environments at home and at work around the theme of weight loss, with the goal of "I want to lose twenty pounds," for example. Encourage your people to work up an environmental engineering plan and include as many stimulating ideas and reminders as possible, such as:

   • Put a sign up on your refrigerator that reads "no high-calorie foods permitted in this area."

   • Add a few pictures of trim people around this sign on your refrigerator. Buy a scale, weigh yourself at the same time each day, and record your weight. Tape up your desired weight at various conspicuous points around your house.

   • Assign a special "my exercise room."

   • Leave some environmental reminders, like "You can do it," to inspire you to go that extra pound.

   • Carry a calorie book with you, and jot down the estimated calories of everything you eat, even the one potato chip.

- Reward yourself with a brand new outfit that will complement your weight loss, instead of a gooey dessert.

Whatever your goal is, start an advertising campaign in your environment.

2. *Put yourself on a diet of positive motivational tapes.*

3. *Read only positive books.*

4. *When you come across inspirational quotes, jot them down.*

5. *Listen to positive music.* Imagine you are feeling really enthusiastic as are drive to a meeting to inspire your membership, and you hear the following imaginary songs:

- *What's the Use in Going On, Nothing Matters Anyway*
- *Nothing Ventured, Nothing Lost*
- *I May Be Paranoid, But that Doesn't Mean People Aren't After Me*
- *You're Born, You Work Like a Dog for a Living, and Then You Die*

How would you feel after being barraged by such negative music? Now imagine that immediately before you speak with your membership, you hear the following imaginary songs:

- *Today Will Be My Day*
- *Born to Win*
- *Together, New Heights*

Second-gear yourself and your people by putting positive music in your environment.

6. *Expose yourself to positive media.* Put everything that your hear into perspective. We all tend to get down on life after reading an article about crime. But the fact is that over 99 percent of the people in North America never go to jail. After watching a news story about a

vandalized house, we tend to generalize based on that isolated example and sometimes get down on life. But the fact of the matter is that over 99.9 percent of homes are not vandalized. (Can you imagine a TV anchorperson saying, "Tonight we'll have action shots of a house that wasn't looted.")

The focus is on the negative because it is rare. As a motivating leader, don't build your philosophy of life on the rare occurrence; it's not scientifically accurate. Expose yourself to positive media and encourage your membership to do likewise.

How can you make use of environmental engineering to second-gear your membership?

Environmental engineering: people environment

_____

_____

_____

Environmental engineering: physical environment
1. Start an advertising campaign (plan).

_____

_____

_____

2. Put yourself on a diet of positive motivational tapes.

_____

_____

_____

3. Read positive books (plans).

_____

_____

_____

4. Think of inspirational quotes you can use (plans).

_____

_____

_____

5. Expose yourself to positive media (plans).

_____

_____

_____

Approach #31: Talking It Up

Talking it up is a leadership approach that deliberately uses uplifting, upbeat, enthusiastic, and hopeful words when speaking to the team.

In their now-classic *A New Guide to Rational Living*, Albert Ellis and Robert Harper unravel the connection between what we tell ourselves affects how we look at things, how we feel about things, and eventually our own words that lead us into either action (find-a-way) or inaction (immobilization). Don't depressed people have a depressing vocabulary? Don't positive people have an uplifting vocabulary and tell themselves things that will propel them onward?

What we tell our team is vital to creating that winning, on-the-move, active, find-a-way feeling. Our words
are the propellants that stimulate the minds of our people
over the hills and the obstacles in the way. After reading
the following group of words, record your feelings exactly
at the moment you finish:

closed	dead	boring
stale	common	decayed
same	lifeless	routine
stagnant	rut	ho-hum

Your reactions or feelings about what the words do for
you:

_____

_____

_____

These are stale, talking-it-down words. Do they generate a down, stale feeling within you?

Now consider the next group of words, and record
your feelings upon completion:

crisp	youthful	ascend
on-the-move	birth	virile
fresh	bigger	debut
uplifting	original	prime
high	new	more

Your reactions to or feelings about these words:

_____

_____

_____

The opti-realistic leader encourages the team to find a way by talking it *up*. Contrast the style of two different leaders to the same situation:

Talking-it-down leader	*Talking-it-up leader*
Things look bad.	We face an exciting challenge ahead of us.
I see you people didn't reach 20 percent of your goals.	Congratulations! You reached 80 percent of your goals.
We might as well pack it in.	Let's go that extra mile and show people what we're made of.
Maybe it can be done.	It can be done, and we are the ones who can make it happen.
We're not as young as we used to be.	We will never be younger than we are at this moment.
Our team is too small to take that on.	The quality, not the quantity, of people we have here is what makes us qualified to face that challenge.
That new restaurant across the street is scheduled to open soon. So on their opening day we will cut back on our orders of meats and other foods. Brace yourself for a tough year.	That new restaurant across the street is scheduled to open soon. Their advertising will benefit us, because much more traffic will pass our way each day, so we're building a bigger sign to get noticed. We have a real advantage because we have a well-established crowd here. After experiencing something new, they'll come back to us because of our quality service.
When you ask for money from the public, be very careful and watch what you say.	Every person you see can be a link in the chain that leads to the final cure for cancer. The more people you see, the more people are given the opportunity to be a part of society's and their own future.

There are many ways of approaching the same challenge with you team. One way is to use language that talks it down, which conveys to the membership the feeling, "What's the use—we're already going as fast as we can go." The alternative approach is to get them into a find-a-way mode by talking it up to mobilize your team. The difference is everything!

What issues is your team now facing with which you can use talking it up to help them find a way?

_____

_____

_____

Approach #32: Sweet Surrendering

Sweet surrendering occurs when the leader persuades the team to accept the things they can't change so as to minimize their frustrations and maximize their energies to change the things they can.

In opti-realistic leadership, the leader uses optimistic approaches like Jonas Salking, environmental engineering, and talking it up and combines them with realistic approaches, the first of which is sweet surrendering.

Sweet surrendering grew out of the work of Bob Power and Joanne Hahn and their discussion of "Resignation or Courage? The Wisdom to See the Difference." The two fellow Adlerians argue that courage is the willingness to change and that change can be a move toward accepting inevitabilities.

On a personal note, sweet surrendering occurs when my dear dad and I canoe through some Pennsylvania rapids. After we do all we can to approach a rocky garden of water, we eventually have to relax and give in, surrendering only to get stronger, losing ourselves to find ourselves.

Sweet surrendering is a leadership approach that

involves facing reality head on, without demanding that it be any other way than the way it is.

Devon is passed over for a promotion at a major oil company. Many thought he was the fair-haired boy in the eyes of top management, but the decision is made to hire someone from outside the company. Devon sees this as a raw deal and unfair. At age 30, he becomes frustrated and bitter about losing a job he thought was his. His attitude ("things are unfair") and his comments ("it's not what you know, it's who you know") make Devon not only unpleasant to be around, but someone who mentally sabotages the success of the supervisor who took "his job." Devon's repeated claims of unfairness and organizational injustice and his negative actions soon result in his being transferred to another division. By age 36, he is actually put into a created job where he can do neither any harm nor any good. A brilliant, sparkling career dies an early death because of Devon's refusal to sweet surrender to reality.

Imagine how different Devon's career could have been if he had been realistic. "I didn't get the promotion, and that's a disappointment to me. But I have a few decades of potential success ahead of me. I'll show top management what I'm made of and that I respect their decision."

When is the moment at which the opti-realistic leader and the membership make the decision to sweet surrender? The organization must ask, "Will our time and energies be more effectively spent with this issue than with another issue?" (Be specific about the other issue). If the conclusion is yes, find a way. If the conclusion is no, sweet surrender.

Are there some issues that you currently face that could benefit from a sweet surrender to free up your energies?

Approach #33: Rational Leading

Rational leading is encouraging the team to think rationally as opposed to irrationally about a situation.

In his study on the characteristics of the healthiest human beings, Abraham Maslow found that one of their ingredients was the ability to see things clearly without a need to twist, distort, or bend them.

> One does not complain about water because it is wet or about rocks because they are hard or about trees because they are green. As the child looks out at the world with wide, uncritical eyes, simply noting and observing what is, without either arguing the matter or demanding that it be otherwise, so does the self-actualized person look on human nature in himself and others (Maslow, 1954).

Imagine the find-a-way power a leader has when he or she helps the membership to face reality as it is and not as it should be (should as defined by them). Energies bogged down by irrational thinking are lost energies. There is an alternative—the rational starting point.

Rational leading grew out of the genius work of Albert Ellis in his book *Executive Leadership: A Rational Approach.* Many earlier philosophers approached the idea of rational leading. For example, the stoic philosopher Epictetus argued 2000 years ago, "No human is free who is not master of his or her own thoughts" and "humans are not disturbed by things, but by the views which they take of things." Later, Marcus Aurelius wrote, "no human is happy who does not make himself so." Emmanuel Kant, an eighteenth-century philosopher, exalted the power of the way we perceive things in his philosophy of phenomenology, which suggests that human behavior is a function of the way people look at things (see Chapter 2).

The rational leader's responses to crises and challenges are effective because (1) the leader dares to see things as they are and then (2) the leader operates harmoniously with the external world to (3) either encourage the team to manipulate the external world or to accept it (sweet surrendering). The rational leader makes every effort to wipe out the frustrating results of irrationality.

What is irrationality? How can you observe it? First of all, irrationality is grandiosity or an exaggerated sense of self-importance. In *You Can Do It,* I wrote:

> People who refuse to face the realities in their lives inevitably become frustrated. Their energies become wasted in directions that are unproductive. People who fail to accept reality suffer from a superiority complex in that they believe that the world was created to personally serve them and to protect them from injustices, frustrations and unpleasantries (L. Losoncy, 1980).

Irrationality is seen when people take events in the universe, such as the economy, society, and other people, "personally." Like the child waiting for Santa Claus to come see "only me," they exaggerate their self-importance. It's almost as if they believe that the sun is no longer the center of the solar system. Instead, they believe, "I am; therefore, things better go my way—or else." This perspective moves a person away from a healthy adjustment to reality and binds up one's energies in despair, anger, or frustration.

The rational leader develops a plan to help the membership overcome or avoid three primary irrational beliefs:

1. We must be perfect in every decision we make and everything that we do or else we must not act, because if we make a mistake, it will be devastating. The whole world will look at us in a condescending fashion and our very existence will be threatened. There won't be a tomorrow for us (notice the exaggeration present in irrational thinking).

2. People must treat us kindly, fairly, and considerately. Not only that, they must act the way we want them to act at all times. If they choose to act the way they want rather than the way we want, it is a personal attack on us. It is a sign that we are losing power and control and a sure clue of our impending demise. Obviously, we are more important than others because we have free will, and we won't allow them to have the same.

3. The universe must make things easier for us and must always make events go our way because the world revolves around us. When things don't go our way, it is a sure sign that the universe is treating us as inferiors, which demonstrates that forever more, not just today, things will go downhill.

Rational leading should help rid the membership of its irrational thoughts, such as (1) we must be perfect, (2) people must act the way we want them to, and (3) the world must be fair to us and act favorably toward us.

In place of these irrational thoughts, the rational leader helps the membership to face reality and develop a plan to solve the crises or surmount the challenges.

Irrational thought	*Rational thoughts and actions*
I messed up that huge order. How can I face the owner tomorrow? I think I'll quit. What an idiot I am.	I made a mistake. I'll immediately do what I can to correct it, explain my error, and tell the owner what I learned from the experience to help me the next time.
My report is due on Friday. Oh well, I have Wednesday and Thursday to get to it. Friday is a long way off.	My report is due on Friday. There is no magic that will do the report for me. I have to do it. It won't be any easier to do tomorrow. Let me do it and get it out of my way and off my mind. It's up to me.

Irrational thought	*Rational thoughts and actions*
I'm late again. It's because of the traffic. The traffic should not have been this heavy today. I'll explain that to the boss.	I'll have to remember how heavy this traffic is, adjust to it, and leave earlier tomorrow. I'll offer to stay fifteen minutes later today since I'm being paid to work eight hours a day.
(Whining) Look at this rain again. Why does it have to rain ten days in a row?	It's raining. I'll just use my umbrella.

Since most people think irrationally, and believe that the events in the universe revolve around them, it is a formidable tasks for a rational leader to help people put themselves into a realistic perspective. It can be done with humor. But no matter how it's done, the rational leader avoids the following six irrational words:

Should	Shouldn't
Ought	Ought not
Must	Must not

Whenever hearing any of these irrational words, which suggest that the world must comply with my *should,* the rational leader simply asks the membership to rearrange the irrational sentence with the question, "What's our plan?"

Which irrational thoughts present the three biggest problems to your team? How can you help your team to find a way to think rationally?

Approach #34: Opti-realistic Leading

Opti-realistic leading employs the best of both worlds—optimism and realism—in inspiring the team.

Most of a team's frustration is the result of one or two basic mistakes in its thinking. The first is the failure to face and accept reality as it is (sweet surrendering and rational leading are needed). The second basic mistake in thinking that produces frustration is the failure to realize all of the alternatives that are available once the team faces and accepts reality. In this case, the team needs Jonas Salking, environmental engineering, and talking it up.

The opti-realistic leader inspires within the membership with a desire to take the best of both worlds—optimism and realism. Let's contrast four different types of leadership styles:

PESSIMISTIC

Unrealistic	*Realistic*
Mental set: Things are terrible now, and they will even get worse.	*Mental set*: We're trapped. There are no answers.
Action: Runs away from reality, sees doom, lives in defense, makes excuses.	*Action*: Faces reality but sees only the negative parts of it. Tends toward sameness.
Result: Carries morale downhill.	*Result*: More of the same, the status quo.

OPTIMISTIC

Opti-unrealistic	*Opti-realistic*
Mental set: "What problems?"	*Mental set*: 1. There's a problem that is a challenge to us. 2. Somewhere there is a solution.

Opti-unrealistic	Opti-realistic
	3. Let's generate alternatives.
	4. Let's find the best alternative.
	5. Let's act.
	6. Evaluate action.
	7. Repeat #1 to 6.
Action: Runs away from reality, sees no problem, and thus doesn't face the issue squarely.	*Action*: Faces reality but sees the positive parts of that reality, uses resources to find a solution, believes that we must do something differently in order for things to change.
Result: Creates a period of temporary unrealistic elation followed by a crash with reality.	*Result*: Adjusts to challenges with new solutions.

Which leader would you want in your organization?

How could you make use of opti-realistic leadership on your team?

_____

_____

_____

Ten Crucial Things to Remember and Ten Practical Things to Do from Chapter 8

1. **Remember:** The difference—the biggest difference—between an average leader and a superior leader is seen not during the good times, but rather during the tough times, so...
   Do: Thrive on crises. Love challenges as an enthused child loves a new puzzle. Convey to your people (1) the realistic facts and challenges and (2) your belief

in their abilities to dig deeper to find a solution to the challenge. Be an opti-realistic leader. Help them find a way.

2. **Remember:** Many people give up when the team faces problems. They conclude that there just aren't any solutions, and they stop looking. The optimistic leader ignites the minds of the membership, so...
    Do: Inspire you people by Jonas Salking them. Communicate an unbending belief that your problems have solutions and that the members of your team are the kind of people who can find them.

3. **Remember:** Just as what we eat affects our bodies, the people we associate with affect our thinking, so...
    Do: Surround yourself with positive, uplifting, find-a-way people in your personal and professional life. Their golden ideas will rub off on you and eventually your team.

4. **Remember:** Your environment affects you, but more importantly, you affect your environment, so...
    Do: Take charge of your environment and influence those things that influence it to keep your enthusiasm and optimism high.

5. **Remember:** Depressed people use depressing language. Angry people use angry language. Those who believe that a challenge is insurmountable immobilize the team by down-talk, but motivating leaders use talking-it-up language, so...
    Do: Use talking it up by speaking in positive, lifting, upbeat language. Use upbeat words with your people. See problems as challenges and obstacles as opportunities to move your people to find a way.

6. **Remember:** Sometimes your people's energies can be better spent on one challenge than another. In that case, it is most appropriate to sweet surrender, so...

Do: Determine with the team the most effective way to spend energies. If the team feels that one challenge would take an inappropriate amount of time, accept the situation as it is by sweet surrendering. Then quickly mobilize their energies to attack the next challenge.

7. **Remember:** Frustration is a result of your people failing to face and accept tough realities, so...
   Do: Be a rational leader who helps people realize that the world doesn't revolve around them. Help develop a more rational view of self, others, and life.

8. **Remember:** The highest reflection of one's unwillingness to face the world rationally is by using *should, shouldn't, must, must not, ought,* and *ought not,* so...
   Do: Whenever you, as leader, hear any of these six irrational words, tell the person to change the sentence to answer the question, "What's my plan?"

9. **Remember:** Unrealistic leaders fall into two categories. The pessimistic unrealist believes that things are terrible now, can only get worse, and there is no hope. The optimistic unrealist ignores the realities of the problems that lie before him or her, so...
   Do: See reality head on, as it is and where it is, neither turning it into a catastrophe nor ignoring it.

10. **Remember:** Realistic leaders fall into two categories. The pessimistic realist sees and faces parts of reality clearly, with most attention on the negative and little on the positive resources in the organization. The glass of water is half empty to the pessimistic realist. The second type of realistic leader is the optimistic realist, who sees reality clearly but also sees hope and holds the conviction that there are solutions to the challenges, so...
    Do: When problems arise, face them as an opti-realist who puts people in second gear.

9

ERASE APATHY AND UNCOOPERATIVENESS ON THE TEAM

People are not born disinterested or apathetic. Nor are they born rebellious or uncooperative. Anyone who has studied young children knows that the physically healthy child wants to create, to belong, and to contribute. What happens along the way to produce the discouraged symptoms of apathy, rebelliousness, uncooperativeness, closed-mindedness, and irresponsibility? In *Turning People On: How to Be an Encouraging Person,* I identified a few techniques of discouragement:

1. Discouragement through domination

2. Discouragement through insensitivity

3. Discouragement through silence

Discouragers Who Use Domination

Some dominators are well-intentioned and want to be helpful. They communicate, "I'll help you with your responsibilities since you might mess up."

A new chef is added to a restaurant, and the old chef, Charles, stands over his shoulder every step along the way. "No, no, you'll kill them with all that seasoning" and "wait until I check the meat before you serve it" are just two of the statements of advice frequently given by the talented old-time chef. The young cook never has a chance to learn by doing. He becomes discouraged and begins to feel, "This is so hard I'll never catch on." He eventually quits.

Unfortunately, dominators tend to get into leadership roles and sometimes unintentionally squelch the ideas of the younger teammates because of their overpowering style.

The high school football coach calls all of the plays for the team; consequently, when the quarterback goes to college, he has no experience in thinking for himself. The college coach, a builder of people (not a builder of the self), couldn't break the dependency the young man had developed on his previous coach. Dominators discourage by "doing for" or "rescuing" rather than empowering their people.

Discouragers Who Use Insensitivity

Insensitivity can be observed when a leader acts as if he or she is better than the team or more important than others because of a role or title. The insensitive leader treats team members as "its" or "producers" rather than people. The insensitive leader is often on an ego trip and overestimates the importance of what he or she does. Frequently, the insensitive leader doesn't even know some of the names of his or her teammates. And in most cases, the insensitive leader is quick to use one-upmanship.

Betty and Larry have a family business selling home products. One day they make twenty-three sales, a personal all-time high. They can't wait to tell Carl, their leader, who enlisted them in the program a few weeks earlier. As Carl listens to the proud couple express their achievement, he cuts them short by pointing out how he once sold not just twenty-three but sixty in one day. Carl goes on to tell them how he did it and never once congratulates them.

Instead of leaving with a feeling of accomplishment, Betty and Larry feel defeated and inferior. "How can we ever top sixty?" Betty asks. "I don't know," her exhausted husband responds. After a proud achievement, the dispirited couple goes home discouraged by an insensitive leader.

Discouragers Who Use Silence

Silence is not golden in leadership when recognition for achievement is involved. The motivating leader does not assume that people know they are doing well. Failure to communicate positive observations may lead to discouragement in people.

A teacher returns a test paper to her student and says, "Well, you failed two tests in a row now" rather than telling the student that last time he failed by thirty points and this time by only three points. The teacher is silent about the progress.

A doctor takes the blood pressure of an anxious man, jots down a number on a piece of paper, and says absolutely nothing to the man about the reading.

"Why should I tell them they're doing a good job?" the steel company foreman says. "That's what they're paid for." The foreman is silent about the workers' performance.

Carolyn works as a nurse in a midwestern state. She feels quite competent in her job there, looks forward to going to work each day, and feels as though she has made quite a contribution to the hospital. Then, she and her husband move to another state. With her excellent references, she quickly secures another nursing position. After only three months, she resigns, because she feels that she is no longer a competent nurse. When asked what she did differently at this hospital that made her incompetent, she replies, "I did everything the same except that no one ever said how I was doing, so I assumed I was performing poorly!" Carolyn is undecided about her career, but she has expressed an interest in areas not related to working around people. Discouragers who use silence are totally aloof to the leadership potential they have but aren't using.

Four goal-directed approaches to motivate your teammates to contribute their ideas are discussed in this chapter:

- Morale analyzing

- Goal centering

- Performing perfection-ectomys

- Crediting

This chapter is especially relevant for dealing with the following specific problems:

1. Lack of confidence

2. Closed-mindedness

3. Fear of change

4. Irresponsibility

5. Apathy

6. Rebellion

7. Uncooperativeness

8. Power struggles

Approach #35: Morale Analyzing

Morale analyzing is sensing the morale of the team.

Apathetic or uncooperative people are dispirited, and the team loses its potential. If a leader wants to assess the perceptions of people, one technique he or she can use is a morale analysis. The morale analysis is a tool to measure the members' level of identity with the team and their perceptions of their contributions.

The leader can ask the following questions and then can analyze the results to develop future plans. The leader can decide whether it would be more effective to conduct the analysis anonymously.

1. *How do you think the team feels about your ideas?*

   • I don't know, they never said.

   • They said they were interested, but I tried to give them some ideas and I never heard anything.

   • I think that if I offered a good idea and they might consider it.

   • They are really interested and give you credit.

2. *How do you feel the team would handle an idea that would be an improvement but was inconsistent with its current beliefs?*

   • I don't know.

   • They haven't listened. I tried and was put off.

   • They would honestly listen and maybe change or would explain why they aren't using it.

   • Other (write in):

   _____

   _____

   _____

3. *Who knows the most about your responsibility or role on the team?*

   • Me

   • Someone at my level

- Someone I report to
- Other (write in):

_____

_____

_____

4. *Can you identify ways that would improve your effec-tiveness in your responsibility?*

   YES ❏   NO ❏

   If yes, what would they be?

_____

_____

_____

5. *Which do you feel is most valued on your team?*
   - Not making mistakes
   - Creating new ideas
   - Achieving goals

The morale analysis will help the leader to see what's going on in the team.

Approach #36: Goal Centering

Goal centering involves helping the teammates to focus on the situation and its solution instead of their egos.

Some leaders focus their compass on the team's goals; other leaders are more concerned with their own egos. Goal centering involves making decisions based upon what's best for the team rather than what's best for oneself.

The ego-centered leader believes	*The goal-centered leader believes*
My ideas must always be the ones that are used. If one of my people makes a suggestion for how to improve something, it is a direct attack on me. And my ego won't allow someone to try telling me that my previous ideas are wrong.	It really doesn't matter whose ideas are used here. The most important thing is that the best, the most efficient, and the most enjoyable ways of doing the job are used. The source of the idea has nothing to do with the value of the idea. The goal is the best idea.

If you can, identify some instances where you are ego-centered and make an alternate plan to motivate your apathetic or uncooperative people through goal centering.

_____

_____

_____

One of the simplest rules of psychology is that the only person who needs to defend is the one who feels threatened. The leader with a poor self-image is the one who needs to defend his or her own ego at the cost of new ideas and better ways.

I saw the best example of how an ego thinker functions while I served as director of admissions and registrar of a Pennsylvania community college. The college administration established a goal of increasing its student enrollment. To meet this goal, one of my plans was to enlist the ideas of the students themselves for the best way to promote the college. I selected a social psychology class. The project I gave them was entitled "Applying the Principles of Social Psychology to Increase Student Enrollment." Put yourself in the excited students' shoes. Your ideas could play a role in achieving a goal for your college.

My previous ideas about marketing a college were insignificant compared to the ideas that the students generated. I was so elated with their practical suggestions that I invited the dean of the school to listen to the ideas of these "turned on" students. This was an error in judgment on my part, to say the least! The ego-thinking dean listened to the first inspired student, who suggested that we form a speaker's bureau. The student explained that the speaker's bureau could be composed of students who would go to parent–teacher meetings and to civic, social, and business groups to discuss the program that the college offered. With arms folded, the dean responded, "It'll never work. I've tried that before. You just can't get your foot in the door of those groups. Those people are looking for exciting speakers who have something to offer." The chin of the student who gave the suggestion dropped from noon to six o'clock. Put yourself in this student's shoes. You worked hard to make a contribution to achieve a goal and you've just been told your idea won't work.

Another student exclaimed, "Then why not invite a famous speaker, someone who has something to offer, to our college and open the lecture to the public? We could have an important political figure, writer, comedian, or even a singer perform here. We could advertise in the newspapers, and when people come to the program, we could pass out literature about the school." The ego-thinking dean rebuffed the idea, concluding that the college couldn't afford it because of its limited budget.

The dean felt threatened. Like an ego thinker, the dean thought that if someone else developed the idea to increase enrollment, it would make her less worthwhile and unneeded. How would you feel if you were in this student's shoes?

Have some fun with this one. Tap your understanding of how to motivate people and their ideas. Imagine that you are the dean of that school. Instead of being an ego thinker, be a goal thinker. See how you could take suggestions like those offered by the two students, expand on their ideas, and reach the goal of increased enrollment. Be a goal thinker.

Consider the suggestion of the first student: "We could form a speaker's bureau composed of our own students and go out into the community to speak to a variety of groups about the programs our college offers." Now, with a totally open, goal-thinking approach, take just two minutes to expand on that student's idea. But remember, don't get ego involved. Put red lights on your ego and green lights on your goal. Dream of the possible. Give the student credit and build on the idea.

What did you come up with in two minutes? If you came up with just one idea, you would be more effective in reaching the goal than the college dean—successful leadership through goal thinking.

The ego-centered leader believes	*The goal-centered leader believes*
If I have a personality clash with another individual in an act of revenge or punishment, I will get back at that person, even if it affects what's best for the team.	The team is bigger than me. And the organization's success leads to my personal success. If I have a personality clash with another person, it is vital that I be objective about that person's contributions. It would be self-centered and narrow to get my therapy here in the workplace at the cost of the lives of the team and the other team members.

The director of purchasing for a small Canadian oil-drilling company was traced to be the major factor responsible for the company losing its advantage over its equal-sized competitors. The ego-centered purchaser refused to deal with a salesman whose company produced a more efficient drill. Yet the competitors were purchasing the new drill, which allowed them to drill faster and cheaper.

Upon examination of the situation, the vice-president found that the director of purchasing had all sorts of excuses as to why the company did not at least consider purchasing the new drill: "It'll never work for us. I don't like the idea right now—we're just too small." Then, one day the real reason came out. "And this salesman (who owned the drill franchise for this area) thinks he can walk in and out of my office without an appointment. I don't put up with that from anybody."

Imagine the vice-president's reaction! The company and all of the employees in the company were affected by one leader who needed ego therapy and used his position to retaliate against another individual.

The goal-centered leader rises above individual conflicts and view people's ideas from a higher, more objective level.

1. Make a determined effort to listen to the ideas of all of your people regardless of whether you like or dislike them personally. It doesn't follow logically that if you dislike someone, then he or she doesn't have anything to contribute.

2. Think big. Make your decisions based on what's best for the team. Be known as a big thinker who doesn't need the leadership position for personal therapy.

Approach #37: Performing Perfection-ectomys

Performing perfection-ectomys is helping the team to develop the courage to be imperfect, to have the courage to create and act without guarantees.

The growing team is constantly in a state of change, adopting, altering, and adjusting to external demands, its own internal needs, and its goals. These changes are frequently resisted by people who have become comfortable with the status quo and are uncomfortable with the new. In many cases, the change resister is a perfectionist who views change as a potential threat because he or she could "do it wrong" the new way.

Other perfectionists appear apathetic, never make contributions or offer new ideas, and panic when making mistakes. People who have difficulty making decisions are saying by their actions, "I'm afraid of doing something unless I'm guaranteed ahead of time that it will be perfect." In each of these instances, resisting change, apathy, fear of mistakes, and unwillingness to make decisions, we see evidence of the underlying disease of perfectionists. They need a perfection-ectomy performed by an encouraging leader.

To perform a perfection-ectomy, a leader must sensitively go to the world of the discouraged person and experience his or her private logic (see Chapter 2). Remember, people operate out of the way they (not I) look at life. After experiencing the private logic, the leader is in a position to more fully understand the perfectionist's private logic. For example, "when I offered a suggestion in the past, some of the other members laughed at it, the boss said it would never work, and I was humiliated, so I'll just keep my idea to myself."

After understanding by transferring to the member's world, the leader performs the delicate surgery by planting the following ideas in the person to remove the perfectionism and replace it with the courage to be imperfect:

1. No idea is wrong. All good breakthroughs were novel ideas at one time. At most, your idea won't be usable.

2. There is not just one right way of doing things, but there are as many ways to look at a challenge as there are people.

3. You are one of a kind. We need your unique input. We may not agree, but after all, if both of our ideas are the same, one of us becomes necessary.

4. The value of an idea is not based upon who suggests it. The value of an idea is based upon its ability to work.

5. Some ideas have value in themselves, and some ideas have value because of their ability to generate other ideas. Don't ignore sharing your idea just because it doesn't appear to have immediate value.

6. Don't wait for the right moment to act. When you think of a new idea, share it.

7. The only bad idea is the one that is not shared. In fact, sharing the idea is more important than the actual content of the idea. Why? Because if a person keeps sharing new ideas, a usable one will eventually emerge. If an individual holds back for fear that the idea may be stupid, nothing new will appear.

The sensitive perfection-ectomy is successful when the member makes the first move to share an idea, shows a willingness to see a new way of doing things, or dares to make a decision and take full responsibility for it. Don't miss the opportunity to celebrate that moment with the person. You played a big role in his or her growth as a team member and as a person.

Who on your team lacks the courage to take a risk and could benefit from a perfection-ectomy? What's your plan?

_____

_____

_____

Approach #38: Crediting

Crediting is the process of giving credit to the teammate who offers ideas to improve the team.

Crediting, like underwhelming in Chapter 4, is limited to a secure leader. Crediting is the process of giving open credit to the person who suggested an idea. Dale Carnegie was a master at giving credit. President Ronald Reagan had a plaque on his desk that read, "No task is impossible to achieve for the man who doesn't care who gets the credit." William Ouchi, author of *Theory Z*, discovered the reason for the impressive productivity of the Japanese worker-trust. Workers who offer their supervisor a new idea trust the supervisor to give them the credit.

Crediting is an effective leadership tool because it fulfills the needs for attention, recognition, and contribution. It also motivates and gives meaning. "That's my idea we are using. I will make sure it works."

Crediting even motivates those who sense that if they share an idea with the leader, their autograph, and not the supervisor's, will be written on that idea.

Some leaders use crediting by assigning to the idea the name of the person who developed it. "We'll call this the Johnson Plan."

Crediting can also be used at regular meetings. For example, the leader informally or casually looks at one of the members and comments, "Jim, you have been telling me this for some time. I now understand what you are saying." Jim has been credited.

A bit of warning here. Be cautious about over-crediting one particular individual and overlooking the accomplishments of others. Sometimes resentments build. Also be sensitive to the results of crediting. For example, teenagers who are credited may be hassled by their peers out of jealousy. In these cases, credit in private. But don't stop crediting.

Rules for Crediting

1. Think of some past ideas and try to tie them to their source. Credit them even though it was some time ago.

2. Never take credit when you can give it.

3. Remember how you felt when someone gave you credit for your ideas in the past. You can now, as leader, give others that same impetus.

4. To really turn someone on, share with your leader, manager, or supervisor that person's idea with credit to him or her Not only will the idea be planted positively when they hear about it, but your leader will be impressed with your style.

   Who can you give credit to today for ideas they gave in the past?

_____

_____

_____

Ten Crucial Things to Remember and Ten Practical Things to Do from Chapter 9

1. **Remember:** Apathetic, uninvolved, rebellious, or closed-minded people are not born that way. They want to belong, contribute, and grow, but they are discouraged, so...
   Do: Show the apathetic person how he or she has something to contribute. Win the rebel over by letting him or her know you could really use their input. Turn closed-mindedness into openness by building pride in the person's growth.

2. **Remember:** Theoretically, every person has ideas for how to improve his or her effectiveness, so...
   Do: Spend a few minutes with each person, the "expert on the job," and create a safe atmosphere that will help the person to think improvement.

3. **Remember:** A sensitive leader is tuned in to the morale and perceptions of the membership, so...
    Do: Consider conducting a formal or informal analysis on how the team feels about the way its ideas are handled. You can use the form in the section on morale analyzing in this chapter.

4. **Remember:** Ego-centered leaders use their position for their own therapy; goal-centered leaders use their position to achieve the team's goals, so...
    Do: Keep personalities out of decisions. Remember that the value of an idea is not based on who gives it, but rather on how effective the idea will be.

5. **Remember:** When someone criticizes you, the criticism is a potential opportunity to grow, so...
    Do: Welcome criticism. It marks you as a leader who wants to improve and be the most effective leader possible. It also marks you as a model to your people, so that when you confront them with class, they will be able to handle it less defensively.

6. **Remember:** You can assess your people's growth potential by observing their openness to new ideas and their desire to improve, so...
    Do: Identify people who handle criticism non-defensively. They may very well be the people to whom you look when making decisions for future advancements. With openness, there is no limit to their growth potential.

7. **Remember:** Change resisters or people afraid of making a mistake or making decisions suffer from perfectionitis, so...
    Do: Perform a perfection-ectomy to remove fear of the new or fear of responsibility.

    1. Go to their world to understand it (transfer).

    2. Communicate "No idea is wrong. There are many ways of doing things. We need your unique input. The value of an idea is not based on who

gives it, but on its ability to work. Some ideas have value because they trigger other ideas, so when you think of a new idea, share it."

8. **Remember:** When someone takes a chance and shares an idea, it is an indication that a successful perfection-ectomy was performed. But the disease can reoccur, so...
    Do: Don't miss the opportunity to acknowledge your appreciation of an idea. Get back to the person. After sharing an idea, the person is waiting anxiously for your opinion. Offer thanks!

9. **Remember:** Some apathetic or uncooperative people have previously shared an idea with a leader who took credit for it. This built distrust and turned them off, so...
    Do: Make crediting an important and regular practice. Think of an idea you recently used and credit the originator again.

10. **Remember:** Psychologists estimate that humans use only two to fifteen percent of their creative potential, so...
    Do: Unleash part of the other ninety percent of your team's ideas by slashing the fear of failure, which is the key mental block to creativity. Be a goal-centered leader and reinspire your apathetic and uncooperative people to be contributing team members.

10

TURN INDIVIDUALS INTO TEAM PLAYERS

*The whole is more than
the sum of its parts;
team power is more than just
the sum of individual efforts.*

The gravelly voiced drill instructor opens up the session at boot camp with the greenies by doing what he always does during the first workout. His goal is to quickly establish the fact that he is the boss and that the pecking order begins with him.

"Let me start off, right here and now, by saying that maybe some of you guys think that you are pretty tough already and don't need this training." As he looks out at the sea of rookies, merely boys, he continues, "Now you see, I'm not that big, but I'll tell you this. I can lick any one of you here. So if any of you tough ones want to show the other boys how you can whip a seasoned sergeant, come up here right now and let these other boys see you eat dirt. Come on, I'll take any one of you on."

Even the breathing stops as the young recruits sit submissively in his scope. The sergeant is so accustomed to this motionless compliance that he could let the moments hang as easily as one counts sheep. As he is ready to move on to the next phase of training, the silence is broken by a man in the next to last row.

As the recruit stands up with all of his at least 300 pounds (mostly above the waist), a pair of unblinking eyes, teeth like a barracuda's, and arms like oil pipelines, he politely blurts out, "Name's Hardrock from Coal City, U.S.A., Sergeant. I'd like to take you up on your challenge."

For a moment, the drill instructor looks as nervous as Don Knotts. Then he quickly transfers all of his muscles to his mind. As recruit Hardrock nears him, the drill instructor, digging for his deepest voice, asserts, "Hardrock, let me have a few words with you." The two huddle, and their caucus ends with the sergeant's right arm over the soldier's shoulder. The sergeant looks out at the other recruits and asserts, stronger than before, "All right, you guys think you're big, don't ya? Well I have news for you. Hardrock here and I will take any two of you!"

The sergeant took one giant step in understanding the importance of team power, but he stopped short. Enlist not only the cooperation of Hardrocks, but help everyone be an empowered, contributing, cooperating team member. When you do, you will experience the potential of team power.

There are a number of reasons why team power is much more effective than individual power:

1. Team power helps all people feel a part of the whole, thus satisfying each person's need to belong and contribute to the team (see Chapter 2 on human needs).

2. Team power rallies a group around a common goal. It unites many individuals by giving them common interests and common achievements to celebrate.

3. Team power instills pride in not only self, but in the whole team.

4. Team power leads to greater involvement and greater understanding of each person's role and how he or she fits into the goals of the team.

5. Team power makes cooperation and mutual encouragement the call words of the day.

Team power is a natural overflow of people as social beings and fulfills the need to belong.

Five approaches to building a team feeling, so that more of the membership will be involved and motivated, are discussed in this chapter:

- Team theming

- Cooperative focusing

- Sociograming

- Welcome mat weaving

- Team esteeming

These approaches are discussed in terms of turning self-centered individuals into team players.

This chapter is especially relevant for dealing with the following challenges:

1. Destructiveness and competitiveness within the membership

2. Uninvolved members

3. Backbiting

4. Cliques

5. Isolates

6. Rejected members

7. Uncooperativeness among different departments

8. Individualism

Approach #39: Team Theming

Team theming is constantly reminding the team to think in terms of team themes by using "we," "our," and "us."

Motivating leaders think in terms of *we, our,* and *us,* not *I* or *me.* They never stray far from the emphasis on the total team. These leaders have a continuous plan to get the membership to think *we,* not *I,* in their actions and decisions. Although this flies in the face of recent cultural trends ("I'm better than him" or "I'm faster than her"), the leader wants everyone to be motivated, not just one or two people. You as leader can help your people to think *us* with an active campaign to promote the theme of team.

Initiate your own advertising campaign for team power. Talk up the importance of team power at staff meetings. Here are some tips to get your campaign rolling:

1. Build a team theme by pointing out how great athletic teams work together by using team power. Use some specific examples of teams that had one great athlete, but didn't succeed because of lack of team cooperation. Drive home the point that no individual ever won the Super Bowl; it was a team effort.

2. Build a team theme by posting signs in the work or family environment to remind your people to think *team.* Just as the food you eat affects your body, the ideas around you affect your thinking. Constant reminders in the environment can help nourish team power thoughts, For example:

   • Think team

   • Does one teammate need a boost today?

   • Give credit

   • We are Super-Bowlers

   • Everyone here is a teammate

   • Cooperate

   Be creative. Add your own relevant messages to the work environment to constantly remind your people to think *team.*

3. Think a team theme in all of your decisions. Be sensitive to how your decisions affect all team members. By constantly giving your toughest challenges to the same person, are you unwittingly creating a one-man band? By constantly acknowledging only one department, are you ignoring a few others, making them feel like they've been snubbed rather than like necessary contributors to the team effort? Think *team* in all of your decisions.

Build a team theme by thinking *we, our,* and *us* in everything you as leader do.

What could you do today to build your team cohesiveness through team theming?

_____

_____

_____

Approach #40: Cooperative Focusing

Cooperative focusing involves emphasizing and rewarding cooperation over competition among teammates.

The encouraging leader who recognizes team power accentuates an atmosphere of allies. Whenever you see an organization with flaring spirit and strong morale, you will find a talented leader behind the scenes. No doubt, one of the approaches the leader uses is an *emphasis on cooperation* and a de-emphasis on competition among team members.

Focusing on cooperation to build team power is a shift from past thinking, when a leader would play one person against another. While competition is a crucial fact of life, your company or organization is competing against other companies. Competition within your own team discourages more people than it motivates. A competitive atmosphere is the antithesis of an atmosphere that builds team power.

Did you ever have a teacher who emphasized competition and gave the top student the first seat, the second best student the second seat, and so on? When some students received recognition, what were the attitudes of the students sitting in the back half of the classroom? Some of the by-products of heightening competition among your teammates include:

1. Claims of injustice, unfairness, and favoritism

2. Blaming ("The test was stupid. The teacher (manager) doesn't care.")

3. Excuses ("If only it wasn't for")

Team power cannot happen when competition is emphasized.

Emphasize cooperation by putting the accent on the times you observe cooperative behaviors. A friend of mine, Dr. Don, made a commitment to tap the potential of team power. Dr. Don, a divisional vice-president of a major U.S.-based steel company, is one of the top metallurgists in the world. In addition to that, he was a leader who put a great deal of energy into helping his five unique departments work together.

While addressing his 400 employees on the concept of team power, I was inspired by Don's opening remarks. Like clockwork, the doctor of metallurgy showed an acute knowledge of human behavior when he recommended, "Look at the power we have when we work together." He cited five specific instances in which cooperation among the five divisions achieved specific results. Don helped 400 highly intelligent men and women to continue working together by taking a few minutes to encourage team power by emphasizing cooperation as opposed to competition. He told the following story about the power of working together.

A person was given the opportunity to observe the

difference between heaven and hell. The person was first taken to hell, where he observed a large banquet hall with delicious food. But no one could eat because their arms were extended straight out and they could not be bent to put the food into their mouths. "The frustration of hell," he thought. "You can see the things you can't have. You are immobilized."

The observer was then taken to heaven. To his amazement, he observed the same delicious food and the same unbending arms. But in heaven, the people had figured out a way to eat. They faced each other and fed each other with their stiff arms. Cooperation was the difference. Cooperation helps people achieve their goals.

Craig D., the manager of a highly successful Mexican restaurant in Maui, Hawaii, is a real leader who knows how to tap the potential of team power. While dinning at the restaurant one evening, I was fascinated by the way the maitre d', the cocktail waitress, the entree waiter, and the dessert waitress worked together as harmoniously as a fine melody. In the course of one meal, we experienced four different people serving us. Each person's arrival at the table was deliciously timed. Having been intrigued by this team harmony, I asked one of the waiters how this atmosphere came to be.

"Oh, Mr. D. loves employees to have the family feeling with each other. He gives us pep talks on being a family. In fact, this month he set up a goal of selling a certain number of desserts and said if we achieve that goal, he will take us all out to dinner!"

It is much more effective for the team members to work together rather than to compete against each other. Craig D. knew it. Emphasize cooperation and turn individuals into team players.

How can you use cooperative focusing as a leader?

_____

_____

_____

Approach #41: Sociograming

Sociograming is a leadership tool to assess the social structure of the team in order to identify leaders, cliques, and mutual relationships for the purpose of bringing in the out and bringing up the down.

A sociogram is an interesting approach that a leader can use to gain information about the social structure of the membership, which will assist in building a greater team feeling. Sociograming grew out of the work of educators who wanted to understand children in the classroom better. Through a sociogram, the teacher could gather information about class leaders, isolates, mutual friends, mutual enemies, and so on and then devise a strategy to develop a more harmonious classroom.

How does a leader construct a sociogram? First, the leader decides to either actually ask the membership about its choice or non-choice of people to work with or hypothesizes what the membership's answers would be if asked. The advantage of asking is that some of the responses may be more accurate. The disadvantage of asking is that the leader may feel uncomfortable.

The leader asks or imagines asking each of the membership two questions:

1. If you were to work on a group project, who would you choose to work with? (positive choice)

2. If you were to work on a group project, is there someone who you would choose not to work with? (negative choice)

The leader then plots the responses:

Name	Positive choice	Negative choice
John	Joe	Jesse
Joe	John	No choice
Jesse	Joe	John
Bob	Joe	Jesse

Name	Positive choice	Negative choice
Tom	John	Bob
Lee	Joe	Bob
Merle	Joe	Bob

Next, the leader constructs a sociogram by putting all of the members' names in a circle. An unbroken line with an arrow is drawn from each chooser to the person who is his or her positive choice. Then a broken line is drawn from each chooser to the person who is his or her negative choice.

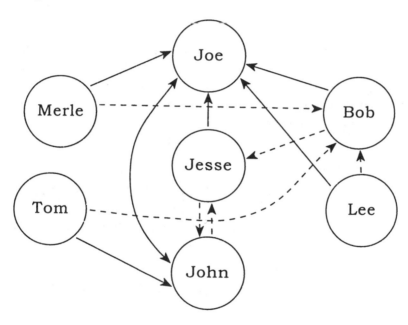

The sociogram reveals the following:

1. Who the leader(s) is(are). The leader is the most frequently chosen teammate (unbroken line). For example, Joe was selected by five people.

2. Who the most rejected teammate(s) is(are). The most rejected person is the one who receives the most negative choices (broken lines). Bob, for instance.

3. Whether there are any isolates in the sociogram. Isolates arc thc people who were neither the positive nor negative choices of anyone.

4. Whether there are any mutual positive choices. Joe and John, for example.

5. Whether there are any mutual negative choices. John and Jesse, for instance.

6. Whether there are any subteams. For example, two leaders who have a following can create two factions, which could lead to competitive disharmony on the team. There are none here.

The leader now has some valuable information to help analyze the patterns that exist within the membership. What are some potential insights that the leader can gather, and what new strategies can the leader employ toward building a team feeling?

Possible Insights

1. Bob may not feel as though he is a team member. In fact, if anything, Bob may be experiencing social problems at work. (Does Bob have an absence or drug- or alcohol-related problem? If so, maybe this is a clue to understanding him.)

2. Merle, Lee, and Tom may not feel as though they are part of the team.

3. Joe is the key to helping build team power because he is sought after and he himself has no negative choices.

4. John and Jesse as a twosome who may require some extra thought.

5. It is possible that John and Jesse are competing for Joe's attention since they both chose Joe and rejected each other? Could jealousies be present? (If so, imag-

ine the devastating cost of heightening the competition between John and Jesse.)

These are just a few hypotheses that would need to be further supported by the leader's observations. Suppose you are the leader of this group and you believe your sociogram and personal observations to be relatively accurate. Imagine that you need to assign people to work together in groups of three, two, and two. Outline a strategy to produce harmonious groups and to maximize membership on the team:

Group A:

_____

_____

_____

Group B:

_____

_____

Group C:

_____

_____

Approach #42: Welcome Mat Weaving

Welcome mat weaving occurs when the leader helps a new member to feel "welcomed" to the team or helps a returning member to feel that his or her absence was noticed.

The motivating leader can weave a welcome mat for new members to welcome them to the team or can extend a welcome back mat to vacationing or disciplined members.

Team power can be built by helping new members who splash into the potentially cold workplace feel accepted by members of the team. The following are some suggestions:

1. Prepare the old-timers for the new person by encouraging empathy for the rookie.

   "Joan, we have a new receptionist starting tomorrow. Her name is Linda and she has a pretty good background in the area of communication, which I know is of interest to you. Would you please take a few minutes to help her feel comfortable with the others here?"

   "Sam, you lived in the Midwest. We have a new receptionist starting tomorrow. Her name is Linda, and she's from Hutchinson, Kansas. Maybe you can help her feel comfortable by talking about some common experiences."

2. Build team power by helping the new people to see who the other cast of characters are and how their work responsibilities intertwine.

3. Empathize the new person's feelings by doing an I-to-you transfer with the new teammate.

4. Help people returning from vacation to feel that their presence was missed.

5. Build total team power by welcoming the disciplined person back to the team and encouraging the other people to do the same.

Build team power by being sensitive to your people's need to feel like a part of the team.

Jot down any instance where you could employ welcome mat weaving with your people in the coming weeks.

_____

_____

_____

Approach #43: Team Esteeming

Team esteeming is building the total "esteem of the team" by uniting them through with their uniqueness, their achievements, their common potential and goals, and their shared vision.

No one doubts the importance of having positive self-esteem. Positive self-esteem gives confidence and is the source of creativity and productivity. It is equally important for team members to have positive team esteem.

Team esteem is built by an asset-focusing leader who rallies around the resources, achievements, and uniquenesses of the membership.

1. *Rallying around the resources of the team*

   • Build team esteem by frequently pointing out all of the vast resources of the total membership.

   • Build team esteem by enthusiastically sharing how each person's resources fit into the total team's resources.

   • Build team esteem by demonstrating your positive expectations of your people based on their vast resources.

2. *Rallying around the achievements of the team*

   • Lift team esteem by never failing to celebrate achievements.

- Build team esteem by showing how far the team has come in its achievements (before and aftering).

- Elevate team esteem by dreaming about and imagining future achievements with the team.

3. *Rallying around the uniqueness of the team*

- Show how this team is special and unique by identifying qualities that this team has that others do not.

- Identify claims-to-fame that highlight the special skills and talents of this unique team.

- Build team esteem by creating nicknames or mottos that reflect a uniqueness (the Whiz Kids, the Fighting Irish).

Ten Crucial Things to Remember and Ten Practical Things to Do from Chapter 10

1. **Remember:** One of the most basic human needs is to belong and contribute to a greater whole than oneself, so...
   Do: Think about each of your people to assess the degree to which his or her need to belong and contribute is satisfied at work. Those who you conclude are not getting their needs satisfied are those who need your intervention to become part of the team.

2. **Remember:** Many people are inclined to think *me* rather than *team* in their actions, and it becomes the responsibility of the leader to develop a plan to change this mental set to *we,* so...
   Do: Initiate an active team power campaign. Talk up the team at your staff meetings. Fill the environment with reminders for everyone to think *team* and to work together.

3. **Remember:** When you heighten the natural competition that already exists among your people, you create more losers than winners. It is a natural psychological process for losers to defend themselves by blaming, making excuses, or claiming that the winner "got all the breaks." Build team power by encouraging cooperation and discouraging competition among your people, so...
   Do: Analyze your everyday "way of being" with your people. Are there times when you play one person against another? If so, be sensitive to finding ways to encourage cooperation among your people.

4. **Remember:** While many leaders make the mistake of believing the way to motivate people is by highlighting competition, the motivating leader knows that highlighting cooperation is a more effective approach to developing all of the people, so...
   Do: Point out cooperative behavior whenever you see it; for instance, one person sharing knowledge, helping, supporting, or encouraging another. The membership will soon realize what the leader values. Be a cooperative focuser.

5. **Remember:** By creating a team theme as opposed to an individual theme, the leader brings in more of the resources of the organization, so...
   Do: Bring in the out, lift up the down, and help everyone to be a contributing team member by team theming everything you do.

6. **Remember:** To build team power, it helps to understand the social structure of your people. One of the most effective tools a leader can use to achieve this is a sociogram, so...
   Do: Construct a sociogram to help identify the leader, the rejectee, the isolates, mutual friends, and mutual enemies. This is an effective way to develop strategies to help everyone to be an involved, contributing member of the team.

7. **Remember:** In the hustle and bustle of your challenges as a leader, it is easy to overlook the feelings of a new person thrown into the organization for the first time, so...
    Do: Be sensitive to a new person and have a plan to help minimize the person's first-day anxieties. Weave a welcome mat for new members.

8. **Remember:** After a person is disciplined or returns from a period of time away, he or she may feel alienated from the team, so...
    Do: Have a plan to welcome people back and make them feel like a member of the team again.

9. **Remember:** Self-esteem is important, as is team esteem, so...
    Do: As leader of the team, build pride through rallying around the team's resources, achievements, and uniquenesses.

10. **Remember:** Most successful teams are not composed of individuals, but instead have people who work together, so...
    Do: Make *team* a regular part of your vocabulary and help everyone feel the pride of that winning touchdown scored by one person, blocked by ten others, and supported and encouraged by the rest of the team.

PRACTICAL
APPLICATIONS

Motivating Leadership Approaches
Applied to Specific Situations

A number of common challenges that the motivating leader faces in the development of a strategy to motivate are listed below. The numbers of some suggested approaches to refer to when building your motivation plan for your team are listed next to each challenge. This section is designed to help the busy leader quickly get his or her hands on some practical ideas without having to page through the entire book. Remember, however, that your own creativity is as important as the ideas on these pages, so create your plan in conjunction with the suggested approaches.

Absenteeism	9, 10, 15, 23, 25, 26, 40
Alcohol problems	2, 11, 15, 23, 25–27, 38
Alienated teammates	1, 6, 9–11, 15–17, 19, 31
Apathy	9–12, 16–19, 24, 35–38, 41

Misunderstandings	1, 3–6, 30, 39–41, 43
Perfectionists	33, 34, 37
Power struggles	see charts in Ch. 2, 1, 3–6, 9, 20, 26, 35, 36, 39, 40
Scapegoats	1, 6, 9–18, 21, 22, 24, 30, 41
Self-centered people	3, 25, 26, 36, 39–41
Stagnation	1, 3, 9, 11, 13, 16, 19, 24
Stubbornness	1, 5, 10, 21, 24, 30, 35, 37, 41
Unappreciated teammates	1, 6, 11–18, 21, 30
Uncooperativeness	1, 3–6, 15–17, 21, 25–27, 29, 38, 41
Violence	1, 4, 9–11, 15, 21, 23–25, 35, 38, 39, 43

Your Team Leadership Motivation Strategy

Specific Challenges (list):

_____

_____

_____

Ideal Leadership Goals (be specific and indicate date initiated and desired date of achievement):

_____

_____

_____

Progress Report:

_____

_____

_____

You Can Be the Motivating Leader!

Mark Twain observed that everyone always talks about the weather but nobody ever does anything about it. Like the weather, everyone talks about unmotivated students, employees, clients, or teammates, but unlike the weather, something can be done about lack of motivation. Unmotivated or irresponsible people are viewed as discouraged. Their discouragement may be seen beneath their apathy, absenteeism, uncooperativeness, rebellion, or myriad other symptoms. Discouraged teammates need encouragement to become turned-on contributing members. They need a motivating team leader.

You can be the motivating team leader who is a positive influence on the lives of the members of your team. You can nurture their potential instead of their excuses and come to grips with the challenges that lie on the path to your goals. When you see disharmony or distrust on the team, you simply build a plan to resolve differences and promote greater understanding. When you see people who are down and out, you develop a strategy to lift them up and bring them in so that they can shine as brightly as possible. When you see alienated, burned-out people who have lost that "first day on a new job" feeling, you light the fires under them with the flames of meaning and purpose. When you see marginal producers, you create a way to communicate high expectations because you believe in them. When you see speed limits being violated, which affects the total membership, you confront with class to build, educate, and steer the problem person back onto the constructive path. When you see people who are overwhelmed by a problem, you inspire the conviction in their minds and hearts that somewhere in their unlimited creativity a solution exists. When you see apathetic and uncooperative people, you win them over with a plan to motivate. When you observe a number of individuals, you become the cohesive glue that ties them together to face the same vision.

When you decide to make a full commitment to be a positive force, at that very moment you acquire a huge advantage over pessimistic leaders. The advantage is that no human achievement has ever occurred because of pessimism or cynicism. Every monumental accomplishment of humankind, from curing polio to placing the American flag on the moon, was the result of the efforts of optimistic, motivated people who were inspired by someone to go on and who refused to quit even in the temporary darkness of night. You can be the motivating team leader who empowers by shining the spotlight on your team's possibilities.

Through your warm lamp of leadership, you bring on the morning, and like the blossoms that decorate the trees in springtime, your team will grow and grow.

And in you teammates' growth, you'll find your autograph.

GLOSSARY OF MOTIVATION APPROACHES

Chapter 3
Positive Leadership Approaches to Resolve Team Differences

Approach #1: Transferring

Transferring involves encouraging people to "transfer" from their own world and walk a mile in their teammate's shoes to understand the other person's own unique responsibilities, pressures, frustrations, and conflicts.

Approach #2: Undiagnosing

Undiagnosing is the process of trying to understand rather than "diagnose," label, or judge a teammate.

Approach #3: Peeking

Peeking is looking under a teammate's surface behaviors, feelings, and beliefs to "peek" at the truer underlying motivations.

Approach #4: De-escalating

De-escalating is a communication tool that resists the natural tendency to judge a teammate as he or she speaks, which escalates the conflict into a win–lose struggle, and instead "de-escalates" by listening in order to understand the other person's feelings about the issue.

Approach #5: Exposing

Exposing occurs when the leader shares his or her pressures, demands, and needs with the team members, thus "exposing" the team to the leader's vantage point.

Approach #6: Linking

Linking is the process whereby the leader points out similarities among the teammates to "link" them closer together in common bonds.

Chapter 4
The Motivating Leader as a People Builder

Approach #7: Re-imaging

Re-imaging involves building teammates by encouraging the development of a more positive self-image. Re-imaging is self-image modification.

Approach #8: Image Analyzing

Image analyzing is analyzing the current self-image of the team or the teammates to uncover perceived strengths and limitations as a starting point for creating a new image.

Approach #9: Asset Focusing

Asset focusing is the process of focusing on a teammate's assets, strengths, and resources to build the person's self-image.

Approach #10: Converting

Converting involves creatively "converting" a person's perceived liabilities, weaknesses, or at first glance negative characteristics into potential assets.

Approach #11: Special-izing

Special-izing is spotting a positive, "special" talent or characteristic in a teammate, such as a "claim-to-fame."

Approach #12: Best Foot Forwarding

Best foot forwarding is centering on a teammate's past or present or visualizing future performance at his or her best rather than at his or her worst.

Approach #13: Un-assuming

Un-assuming occurs when the leader recognizes and shows appreciation for the everyday, routine work of the team rather than "assuming" or taking performance for granted.

Approach #14: Underwhelming

Underwhelming occurs when the leader shares how he or she has grown from the ideas of the team. Underwhelming is the opposite of overwhelming.

Chapter 5
Plant Positive Purpose in People

Approach #15: Home-ing In

Home-ing in is sensitively understanding a teammate's outside-of-work context at home as a factor in the person's attitude and performance.

Approach #16: Meta-job Describing

Meta-job describing involves giving people greater purpose and meaning by reframing their contribution to their own professional development, to their team, to the organization and to the world.

Approach #17: Winding Up

Winding up occurs when the leader gets the team enthused about the day's potential achievements.

Approach #18: Before and Aftering People

Before and aftering people is the process of showing a teammate or the team where they were in the past (before) and how they have progressed to where they are now (after).

Approach #19: Un-meanializing

Un-meanializing is the leader's constant reminder to the team members about the importance of their work and how it fits into the growth of the organization.

Chapter 6
Create a Winning Team Feeling

Approach #20: Respect-ability

Respect-ability is communicating to a teammate or the team "I believe in you. You can do it."

Approach #21: Delegating

Delegating involves constantly analyzing teammates to sense who would be capable of taking on higher level responsibilities, training them, encouraging them, and then celebrating their achievements with them.

Approach #22: "Can" Opening

"Can" opening is a leadership approach designed to create a winning feeling in a teammate by showing the person that he or she has much more potential than they previously thought.

Approach #23: Expectation Altering

Expectation altering involves enhancing one's leadership expectations of a teammate or the team.

Approach #24: Changing Spotlights

Changing spotlights involves putting the "spotlight" on a previously overlooked teammate.

Chapter 7
Confront with Class: Picking People Up Without Stooping Down

Approach #25: Speed Limiting

Speed limiting is a preventive technique that a leader uses to define limits ahead of time for the purpose of maximizing the freedom of the total team. Setting speed limits also reduces anxiety by clarifying rights, responsibilities, and roles and aligning expectations.

Approach #26: Asserting

Asserting occurs when the leader confronts a teammate who violates the speed limits. Assertive leadership is a healthy balance between timid leadership and aggressive leadership.

Approach #27: Disciplining

Disciplining with class is a specific five-step process used by the assertive, encouraging leader to deal with offenders of the team's speed limits.

Approach #28: De-hiring

De-hiring is the process of breaking the ties with a teammate who has continuously violated the rules of the team's speed limits and who has not responded positively to other motivational approaches.

Chapter 8
Inspire Your Team to Find a Way

Approach #29: Jonas Salking

Jonas Salking occurs when the leader inspires the team to operate based on the conviction that problems have solutions.

Approach #30: Environmental Engineering

Environmental engineering is the process of consciously engineering both the social and physical environments in positive ways in order to give the team a lift.

Approach #31: Talking It Up

Talking it up is a leadership approach that deliberately uses uplifting, upbeat, enthusiastic, and hopeful words when speaking to the team.

Approach #32: Sweet Surrendering

Sweet surrendering occurs when the leader persuades the team to accept the things they can't change so as to minimize their frustrations and to maximize their energies to change the things they can.

Approach #33: Rational Leading

Rational leading is encouraging the team to think rationally as opposed to irrationally about a situation.

Approach #34: Opti-realistic Leading

Opti-realistic leading employs the best of both worlds—optimism and realism—in inspiring the team.

Chapter 9
Erase Apathy and Uncooperativeness on the Team

Approach #35: Morale Analyzing

Morale analyzing is sensing the morale of the team.

Approach #36: Goal Centering

Goal centering involves helping the teammates to focus on the situation and its solution instead of on their egos.

Approach #37: Performing Perfection-ectomys

Performing perfection-ectomys is helping the team to develop the courage to be imperfect, to have the courage to create and act without guarantees.

Approach #38: Crediting

Crediting is the process of giving credit to the teammate who offers ideas to improve the team.

Chapter 10
Turning Individuals into Team Players

Approach #39: Team Theming

Team theming is constantly reminding the team to think in terms of team theme, by using "we," "our," and "us."

Approach #40: Cooperative Focusing

Cooperative focusing involves emphasizing and rewarding cooperation over competition among teammates.

Approach #41: Sociograming

Sociograming is a leadership tool to assess the social structure of the team in order to identify leaders, cliques, and mutual relationships for the purpose of bringing in the out and bringing up the down.

Approach #42: Welcome Mat Weaving

Welcome mat weaving occurs when the leader helps a new member to feel "welcomed" to the team or helps a returning member to feel that his or her absence was noticed.

Approach #43: Team Esteeming

Team esteeming is building the total "esteem of the team" by uniting them through their uniqueness, their achievements, their common potential and goals, and their shared vision.

BIBLIOGRAPHY

Adler, Alfred. *Understanding Human Nature.* New York: Greenberg Publishers, 1927.

Alberti, Robert E., and Michael Emmons. *Your Perfect Right.* San Luis Obispo, California: Impact, 1982.

Ansbacher, Heinz, and Rowena Ansbacher. *The Individual Psychology of Alfred Adler.* New York: Basic Books, 1956.

Bennis, Warren. *The Unconscious Conspiracy: Why Leaders Can't Lead.* Executive Books, 1978.

Cahn, Richard. Personal communication, January 1994.

Channon, Jim. "Creating Esprit de Corps," in *New Traditions in Business.* San Francisco: Berrett-Koehler, 1992.

Crosby, Philip. *Quality Is Free.* New York: McGraw-Hill, 1979.

Csikszentmihaly, Mihaly. *Flow: The Psychology of Optimal Experience.* New York: Harper & Row, 1990.

Dinkmeyer, Don, and Lewis E. Losoncy. *The Encouragement Book.* Coral Springs, Florida: CMTI Press, 1995.

Ellis, Albert. *Executive Leadership: A Rational Approach.* Citadel Press, 1978.

Ellis, Albert, and Robert Harper. *A New Guide to Rational Living.* North Hollywood, California: Wilshire Books, 1975.

Ferguson, Marilyn. *The Aquarian Conspiracy.* Los Angeles: Tarche Books, 1980.

Frank, Jerome. *Persuasion and Healing.* Baltimore: Johns Hopkins, 1961.

Gatto, Rex P. *Teamwork through Flexible Leadership.* Pittsburgh: CTA Press, 1992.

Hall, Jay. *Teamness Index.* Woodlands, Texas: Teleometrics International, 1988.

Harding, K.L.A. "A Comparative Study of Caucasian Male High School Students Who Stay in School and Those Who Drop Out." Ph.D. dissertation, Michigan State University, 1966.

Hawley, Jack. *Reawakening the Work Spirit.* San Francisco: Berrett-Koehler, 1993.

Losoncy, Diane. "The Effects of a Team Mutual Encouragement Skills Training Program on Teamness and Social Self-Concept," unpublished research article, 1994.

Losoncy, Lewis. *Teamwork Makes the Dream Work.* Solon, Ohio: Matrix Essentials Press, 1994.

Losoncy, Lewis. *Think Your Way to Success.* North Hollywood, California: Wilshire Books, 1982.

Losoncy, Lewis. *You Can Do It.* New York: Simon & Schuster, 1980.

Losoncy, Lewis. *Turning People On.* New York: Simon & Schuster, 1978.

Maltz, Maxwell. *Psycho-Cybernetics.* North Hollywood, California: Wilshire Books, 1960.

Maslow, Abraham. *The Farther Reaches of Human Nature.* New York: Viking Press, 1971.

Maslow, Abraham. *Motivation and Personality.* New York: Harper & Row, 1954.

May, Rollo. *Freedom and Destiny.* New York: Norton, 1981.

McFarland, Lynne Joy, Larry E. Senn, and John R. Childress. *21st Century Leadership.* New York: The Leadership Press, 1993.

Mears, Peter, and Frank Voehl. *Team Building.* Delray Beach, Florida: St. Lucie Press, 1994.

Moore, Thomas. *Care of the Soul.* New York: Harper, 1992.

Naisbitt, John. *Megatrends.* New York: Warner Books, 1982.

Parker, Glenn. *Team Players and Teamwork.* San Francisco: Jossey-Bass, 1990.

Peters, Tom, and Robert Waterman. *In Search of Excellence.* New York: Warner Books, 1984.

Purkey, William. *Self-Concept and School Achievement.* Englewood Cliffs, N.J.: Prentice-Hall, 1970.

Rogers, Carl R. *On Becoming a Person.* Boston: Houghton-Mifflin, 1961.

Schwartz, David. *The Magic of Getting What You Want.* New York: William Morrow, 1983.

Seligman, Martin. *Learned Optimism.* New York: Knopf, 1991.

Whyte, William. *The Organization Man.* New York: Toplinger Publishing, 1972.

Wilson, Colin. *New Pathways in Psychology.* New York: Toplinger Publishing, 1972.

Zogas, Gust. Personal communication, January 1994.

INDEX